NOV 03 2021

D1175236

THE MODERN TIFFIN

The MODERN TIFFIN

ON-THE-GO VEGAN DISHES WITH A GLOBAL FLAIR

PRIYANKA NAIK

TILLER PRESS

New York   London   Toronto   Sydney   New Delhi

TILLER PRESS

An Imprint of Simon & Schuster, Inc.
1230 Avenue of the Americas
New York, NY 10020

First Tiller Press hardcover edition November 2021

TILLER PRESS and colophon are registered trademarks of Simon & Schuster, Inc.

For information about special discounts for bulk purchases, please contact
Simon & Schuster Special Sales at 1-866-506-1949 or business@simonandschuster.com.

The Simon & Schuster Speakers Bureau can bring authors to your live event.
For more information or to book an event, contact the Simon & Schuster
Speakers Bureau at 1-866-248-3049 or visit our website at www.simonspeakers.com.

Interior design by Matt Ryan
Photography by Melissa Hom
Food styling by Julia Choi-Rodriguez
Illustrations by Jennifer Xue

Manufactured in China

10 9 8 7 6 5 4 3 2 1

Library of Congress Cataloging-in-Publication Data
Names: Naik, Priyanka, author.
Title: The modern tiffin : on-the-go vegan dishes with a global flair / Priyanka Naik.
Description: New York : Tiller Press, [2021] | Includes index. | Summary:
"Champion the diversity and versatility of vegan cooking with these
delicious, unique recipes sure to break the mold"—Provided by publisher.
Identifiers: LCCN 2021005819 (print) | LCCN 2021005820 (ebook) |
ISBN 9781982177089 (hardcover) | ISBN 9781982177096 (ebook)
Subjects: LCSH: Vegan cooking. | Cooking, Indic. | LCGFT: Cookbooks.
Classification: LCC TX837 .N264 2021 (print) | LCC TX837 (ebook) | DDC 641.5/6362—dc23
LC record available at https://lccn.loc.gov/2021005819
LC ebook record available at https://lccn.loc.gov/2021005820

ISBN 978-1-9821-7708-9
ISBN 978-1-9821-7709-6 (ebook)

To Maa, Dad, Kirti, and Puja . . .
and to myself, because who am
I kidding? I've been working way
too hard not to!

In memory of our Aai, who passed
on generations of technique, delicious
food, and love through our mom

Shanta Devi Kore
September 14, 1935–October 19, 2020

CONTENTS

CONTENTS

❧❧❧

INTRODUCTION

I t was a crisp fall day and I remember the smell of fragrant masalas warming up the house while I sat at the dining table . . . refusing to eat my food. Yup, there I was, giving my mom a hard time about eating my dinner. I would be the first to sit at the dinner table to start eating and the last to leave—I wasn't allowed to get up until every bite was finished. (My family always wondered how I had such chubby, pinchable cheeks when I barely ate. But I digress.) Although I was a stubborn girl who refused to eat, what I didn't forget was my mom's creativity and dedication to feeding us delicious and healthy vegetarian food. Neither I nor my two older sisters would leave the house without a packed lunch—and I'm not talking about a bologna sandwich or a Lunchables kit. I'm talking about eggplant parm mini heroes; Bombay sandwiches, layered with fresh chutney, seasoned potatoes, and cucumbers; and spaghetti with homemade spicy cheese sauce flavored with Indian masalas, paired with a Frooti mango juice—all packed in a segmented lunch box, so as to not compromise each delicious component, similar to a *tiffin* (see page 6).

Traditionally, a tiffin is a two- or three-layered, stacked steel lunch box intended to separate each component of a meal. So you can have your rice or chapati in the first layer, a vegetable masala dish in the second, and a daal (stewed lentils) in the third layer. The concept helps retain the integrity of each dish and helps in maintaining how Indian food is traditionally eaten—each component separate, not mashed up together in a bowl. My mom would pack our lunches in similar lunch boxes, but rather than being stacked, they were segmented school lunch boxes. Lunchtime was always my most anticipated period during the school day—just thinking about opening up each section of my lunch box to unveil a tasty surprise was much more interesting than social studies.

In addition to taking our Indian-inspired packed lunches, we never left the house without saying a quick *pooja* (prayer) in our Hindu temple. As a first-generation Indian American growing up on Staten Island, it could have been easy to completely assimilate into American culture and lose touch with my Indian heritage and roots. But my parents made sure that did not happen, by teaching us our native language of Kannada, taking us to India every year, and most importantly, teaching us about our culture through food.

Life is funny. As I grew older, I began to appreciate the food my mom made, specifically her creativity with vegetarian dishes, and the fact that there were endless possibilities. As soon as I hit middle school, I was packing my own lunches—big girl now!—and eagerly cooking with my mom in the kitchen, while obsessively watching cooking shows. Some of my favorites included *Good Eats* with Alton Brown and the OG *Iron Chef* with the Chairman, Takeshi Kaga. The rush of excitement and adrenaline while watching cooking competition shows was unlike anything else for me. What are they doing to that appetizer? Are they really using the squash like that? That was not a good enough dish to win, come on! You get my drift.

My interest in cooking became more serious when the representatives from Johnson & Wales and the Culinary Institute of America visited my high school on Staten Island. I met with them and thought on enrolling long and hard. Ultimately I made the decision not to go. You're probably dying to know why, right? First: I was not fully comfortable with the prospect of having to cook and eat meat—I rarely ate chicken and seafood and was not interested in expanding my nonvegetarian intake at that time of life. Second: culinary school was very expensive, and I found it peculiar that there were no preprofessional courses offered in addition to the culinary courses. So, if I wanted to start a business or enter into a different profession outside of cooking, they didn't prepare you for that. And third (and probably the most important for me): culinary school is European-based and teaches the most "Westernized" standard in cooking. Through my research, I found that most culinary schools spend only a few days on "Asian cuisine." Can you imagine trying to learn ALL of Asian cooking in a matter of three or four days? I don't even know 100 percent of all of my mom's recipes, and that's from only one tiny part of India! My love for cooking was rooted in my heritage, so it wouldn't make sense for me to enter an institution that didn't focus on helping me hone those skills. So, for all those reasons, I opted out of going to culinary school and instead continued working on my skills independently.

My affinity for cooking turned more serious when I became a full-time vegetarian, about thirteen years ago. I often dined out in New York City, informed the host-waiter that I am a vegetarian, and they would promptly point me to the salads or side dishes on the menu. I would think to myself, "What am I? A rabbit?! I have never grown up eating a salad as a meal!" That's when it occurred to me—it's not their fault, it's just that the Western world is not aware of all the amazing dishes that can be created simply out of vegetables!

In order to break the mold of the Western plate: meat, potatoes, vegetable, I started a blog to showcase all of the dishes that anyone can make using vegetables. At the time, I used the only public social media platform available—Twitter—to share my recipes. From there, my original creations were featured on PETA, Meatless Monday, and across several brand profiles. My obsession with wanting to showcase all the cool and accessible possibilities with vegetarian cooking didn't stop there. I went so far as to incorporate this obsession into every corporate job I had: I started a "Bread-Off" baking challenge while at Publicis Groupe and pioneered a Bloomberg Pantry Social Account while at Bloomberg LP, sharing all the meal possibilities using their pantry snacks and ultimately becoming an official account for Bloomberg LP. All the while, I was packing my lunch every day for work, similarly to how my mom packed us lunches when I was a child on Staten Island, in segmented lunch boxes.

I knew I had to do more to prove my credibility in the food industry. As a self-taught cook who is not a food writer full-time for a major publication, the climb is that much steeper. I began trying out for *Food Network Star* by attending open casting calls and after two failed attempts, I reevaluated my approach. What story was I trying to tell? All of my recipes were vegetarian, the majority vegan, but there wasn't a clear connection between my present-day life and my upbringing. And that's when I realized that most of the recipes I was creating were subconsciously associated with my childhood and consciously associated with my current work and travel life. For instance, one of the most popular dishes from my blog at the time was my One Pot Edamame Pasta with Coconut-Turmeric Sauce (a recipe I had been making since 2016, but only posted in 2018 after much testing!). This dish was inspired by the coconut-based curries I indulged in while traveling through Thailand in 2016; my love for Italian pasta as a Staten Island native; and my inclination to use turmeric, because let's be honest, every Indian dish we ate growing up at home had turmeric! And that's when it hit me—my style of cooking is not just vegetarian or vegan, it's a culmination of my heritage and travels, making for Indian-inspired global dishes.

Redemption. In 2016, I discovered the Food Network show *Cooks vs. Cons*, where four contestants (two amateur and two professional cooks) battle it out to win the title of best cook, and auditioned. This time I had a clear story on who I was and what my cooking style was. Finally, in 2017, I was cast for Season 5, Episode 12, and competed with an all-vegetarian menu and won! The episode was actually named after something I said in the interviews: "I'm nacho average cook."

This achievement helped put my food and story on the map—I have since won *Dishmantled*, a fierce cooking competition hosted by Tituss Burgess; been a featured chef on NBC's *TODAY* show; a host on an original show on Tastemade Streaming Networks called *Dish It Healthy*; have starred in campaigns for Amazon, Coca-Cola, and the like; hosted several pop-up dinners around New York City; and was the first Twitter employee to guest chef in New York and San Francisco, serving over two thousand people a custom-curated menu of my original dishes, and have been interviewed and featured in *Forbes*, CNN, *GQ*, and more, on my original vegan cooking style.

My story isn't finished. After my nearly ten-year food journey, while having a full-time career in tech and traveling to nearly forty countries, there are a few things that I've learned to practice in my day-to-day to make my life easy: portioning all of my recipes for two people (but they can be easily scaled up to feed four), ensuring that everything I cook is portable, putting my health first (that means no dairy, butter, ghee, or deep-frying), progressing to an all-vegan diet, and trying my best to cook sustainably. As a millennial living and supporting myself in Manhattan, while building on my dreams, all of these aspects are essential in helping me stay healthy, giving me a creative outlet, and living my best veggie life. This cookbook is not only the first time that I'll be sharing my food journey and story, but also these values of cooking.

The Modern Tiffin will provide you with dozens of Indian-inspired, global dishes that are portable, vegan, portioned for two, and will seamlessly fit into your lifestyle. I hope to inspire your daily routine, changing the way you think about food—breaking that Western-developed mold of a "balanced meal" of meat, potatoes, and vegetable on the side— and rather, opening your tiffin lunch at work and taking a big bite out of your Masala Chickpea Bruschetta, immediately transporting you to the Mediterranean coast of Italy with a surprising Indian kick to perk you up! So, your question shouldn't be, "Oh, where should I order lunch or dinner from today?" but rather, "Where am I traveling today for lunch?"

So, thank you, baby Priyanka, with your stubbornness and chubby-cheeked face. Even though you refused to eat back then, you made me appreciate not only the skill and creativity of my mom's cooking, but also my heritage.

I hope to share a bit of my life with you through *The Modern Tiffin* and bring you along on my food journey. This is only the beginning.

XOXO,
Priyanka

T*he Modern Tiffin* was born from the memories of my childhood, carrying compartmentalized lunch boxes filled with Indian-inspired dishes cooked by my mom. A little Bombay sandwich paired with a Frooti Mango Drink was not a typical school lunch at P.S. 5 on South Shore, Staten Island, where most kids brought in Lunchables, nor was it accepted; my sisters and I were often teased for our weird-looking lunches. But here's to breaking those stigmas and sharing the value of tiffin meals with the world!

The concept of Indian tiffins is not well known or imitated in the Western world but deserves greater recognition and broader adoption, because it's a fun and enticing way to enjoy healthy and tasty cuisine on the go. Traditionally, most Indian meals have several components: a carbohydrate (either a chapati or rice or both), one or two vegetable-based dishes (like stuffed baby eggplant or chana masala, for example), and a soup or stew-like dish like daal (a stewed and spiced lentil-based dish). These components are meant to be eaten together, while still retaining their integrity separately. You will *rarely* see all of these components piled onto one plate and mixed together—it is almost sacrilegious! A tiffin, with its separate compartments, enables the separation of the dishes, while maintaining portability and the ability to consume them together when you've arrived at your destination. The concept helps retain the integrity of each dish, while maintaining how Indian food is traditionally eaten.

But it doesn't stop there. In India, there are "tiffin-wallahs," designated delivery personnel who pick up a tiffin every morning from your home, strap it to the back of their bike, and bike it downtown to hand-deliver to you at your office. Now, I don't expect anyone to strap a tiffin to their bike, but wouldn't it be cool to have that option? So when you're not tethered to your desk or home, you can take your meal with you anywhere!

Tiffins are a part of most Indian families' homes and are passed down from generation to generation. In my possession right now, I have two tiffins: one that originally belonged to my oldest uncle on my father's side and one that was given to my mom when she got married. How do I know? Because tiffins are, of course, engraved for that personal touch! Now that you've read this—can we make tiffins a "thing" in this part of the world? 'Cause I am sure ready to!

MY FOOD PHILOSOPHY

I mentioned earlier that I became a vegetarian about thirteen years ago. Many people assume that I became vegetarian for religious reasons because they take one look at me and think, "You're Indian, so you must be Hindi (they mean Hindu), so you don't eat meat, right?" Whoever assumes this isn't completely incorrect. A large majority of Indians—over 80 percent—are Hindu. And generally, Hindus are vegetarian because the philosophy of Hinduism involves respecting all beings and most, if not all, living beings are represented as some Hindu deity or avatar. I am Hindu and I do practice many of the spiritual and philosophical teachings of Hinduism, but that is not the only reason why I went full-time vegetarian.

In college, I began doing research on the meat industry after reading Michael Pollan's *The Omnivore's Dilemma* (I highly recommend this book if you haven't already dabbled in it). This book piqued my interest in better understanding where my food actually comes from, especially in America, and how we, as humans, have evolved into consuming it versus how we were biologically meant to eat food. Long story short, after doing far too much research, watching many documentaries and one too many PETA videos, I made the decision to cut meat from my diet completely cold turkey. To be honest, I was never a huge fan (eating only chicken and seafood at times) and never craved it—I like vegetables way more. I love animals far too much to be a cause for their harm. Why are my pets, pug Uglee (yes, that was his name) and shih tzus Romeo and Juliet, different from any other animal on this planet? Why is one kind of animal harmed for food and one bred for love?

So, how has all this research and background shaped my food philosophy? I believe we should treat every being as we would want to be treated, and I mean *every* being. We are all on this planet for a purpose, and I think respecting one another is so important. Every being is essential for our ecosystem to flourish and thrive, which, by the way, we are doing a terrible job of sustaining. This is why I evolved into cooking all vegan for more than three years now—because it's not just meat, but also dairy, eggs, palm oil, fashion, travel; so many industries are contributing to the detriment of animals and the environment. If I can share the wealth of knowledge I've learned on how to make delicious food without harming any being around us, why not share it? If I can share what I've learned by living in America and traveling around the world, why not share it? The possibilities of what you can eat are just as delicious, satisfying, and most importantly, good for *you* without putting another life at stake.

I hope my food philosophy opens your minds and palates to all the delicious and cruelty-free possibilities out there, because animals are far too cute, loving, and essential for us and our planet to put on a plate as a hunk of unnecessary meat. Don'tcha think?

TRAVELING THE WORLD

This section of my introduction may sound pretentious: Oh, look at me, just traveling the world on my free time, la-di-da! I know how this sounds, trust me. But if you want to understand the full background of my cookbook, then you have to understand this large part of my life. Since infancy, I grew up traveling to India nearly every year of my life. My whole family, with the exception of my immediate family, lives in India, so it was essential for us to travel there to stay connected to our family and roots. And, fortunately, my family had the opportunity to travel.

But it didn't stop there. We traveled somewhere different nearly every other year, from Alaska to Hawaii to a full European tour and Mexican adventure—we touched quite a few places! Traveling not only offered new adventures of exploring a destination, but also allowed me to immerse myself in different cultures and foods. These childhood experiences gave me the itch to travel at a young age.

This brings me to today. Over the last four or five years, I set a personal goal to travel to at least two or three new countries a year, which meant spending efficiently throughout the year to save for travel and coming up with creative ways of traveling, for instance traveling to a destination where I might have a friend temporarily living or crashing my sister's work trips (ha, sorry, Kirth!). Either way, I found a way and I'm happy to report that I have traveled to thirty-seven countries—it would have been forty in 2020, but we all know how that year went. So in addition to my travels growing up, I have now added Australia, Japan, Thailand, Central Mexico, Spain, Portugal, and Central America to the list—some of which you will find direct influences from in this book!

My travels have greatly influenced my outlook on food, culinary senses, and, most importantly, inspiration for my everyday dishes. Not only are the recipes different in other countries outside of America, but the method and style of eating is different, too. For instance, street food is huge in every Asian country—most diets include many of these delicious and cheap street eats, generally made with local fresh ingredients. Also, the concept of a "balanced plate," containing a giant hunk of protein at the center with carbs and veggies on the side, is nowhere to be found outside of America. Finally, the quality of ingredients vastly differs from what is available in America.

These culinary aspects of exploring different countries fascinate me and have hugely influenced my continued love for cooking and eating. And so, each chapter within *The Modern Tiffin* explores a country and culture that I have traveled to and/or regularly grew up experiencing. I hope each chapter brings you on a journey with me and that you're able to relive some of my favorite travel moments through food.

What's next on my list of travels? Well, I guess you'll just have to keep following my journey to find out!

TIPS & TRICKS
GETTING THE BASICS RIGHT

WHERE TO BUY A TIFFIN

Given the name of this book—*The Modern Tiffin*—you're probably wondering, "Where can I buy a tiffin?" The answer is—many places! If you're interested in living out the portability feature of this cookbook, you can certainly do so by leveraging a classic Indian tiffin, and you can find these steel tiffins at any South Asian or Indian supermarket, and even online. But, if you're looking for something a little *modern*, pun intended, some of the brands I love have created sustainable and portable food wares. Klean Kanteen and Prep'd by Tastemade are two of my favorite modern tiffins available to purchase online. However, if you're trying to live that zero-waste life, then the most accessible "tiffins" are your takeout containers. Yup! I reuse any container I get with a delivery or takeout order and give all of them a new life. It's a great way to repurpose already existing containers, minimize the use of plastic production, and it's much more financially sustainable. Talk about modern, sustainable, and economically efficient tiffins!

FAVORITE TOOLS IN MY KITCHEN

I'm going to let you in on a little secret: I don't have many fancy gadgets in my kitchen. It's true! I'm a simple chef and I take pride in that. I don't think one needs many fancy tools to make a delicious and uniquely flavored meal. But I do have my favorites, and some of them are essential for this cookbook. Here goes!

MORTAR AND PESTLE: This is by far my favorite tool in the kitchen, and in my opinion, one of the most versatile. It can grind dry or wet spices and make chutneys, pestos, and everyone's beloved guacamole. I use a mortar and pestle to grind my dry whole spices throughout this book (and to make my

Mexican Mango Gazpacho) because it allows the slow release of the natural oils and flavors from the whole spices, allowing for a more bold, vibrant, and flavorful dish. My recommendation is to use a marble or stone mortar with a heavy pestle so it can do most of the work for you (with less effort on your part!). At my parents' home, we use a traditional black stone mortar and pestle, which Maa brought over from India (it took up one checked bag!), and I use a heavy white marble mortar and pestle at my home—a *modern* mortar and pestle ;).

TRADITIONAL COCONUT GRATER: When I was growing up, my parents brought home fresh mature coconuts from the Indian temples or grocery stores, cracking them open in the backyard, quickly drinking the coconut water, and then grating each half against our traditional coconut grater. This grater—also a gadget brought over from India—is a slab of wood fit with a spherical serrated blade. You place the coconut half, flesh side down, against the blade and rotate with the handle until all of the meat is finely grated. We'd then pack the coconut into freezer bags and freeze until we needed to use it. Fresh coconut has a short shelf life, which is why we immediately freeze it to preserve the freshness. Grated coconut can last in the freezer for months, up to a year. This grater is not *essential* for this cookbook, but it sure is neat. It's a staple in our family household that I hope Maa passes down to me! For now, I use the good-quality fresh frozen grated coconut that is so readily available.

MICROPLANE: The Microplane fine grater is a key tool in my kitchen. I use it to grate citrus, nutmeg, ginger, garlic . . . the list goes on. It's a fantastic way to add bold flavors in an even and finely grated manner, so they can evenly incorporate into a dish and no one receives a giant piece of ginger, garlic, or citrus in their food.

FOOD PROCESSOR: Don't be shocked, but I do not own a Vitamix. That's right. I do most, if not all, of my blending in a food processor. My recommendation is to get a good-quality food processor with dual blades that has chop, puree, and pulse modes. This allows for the easy production of smooth and creamy sauces, chunky chutneys or salsas, and even dry chutneys and seasonings.

IMMERSION BLENDER: The best handy tool in the kitchen, pun intended! I love having an immersion blender on hand, because it's an easy way to blend sauces directly in a pan or pot, without having to transfer it to a blender. It also provides the flexibility to blend a sauce just slightly, if you want a more rustic feel. This tool is perfect for the Mango Gazpacho recipe on page 126.

STAND MIXER: It should be no surprise to you that I love desserts, cakes, and anything deliciously sweet, which means I have a stand mixer and you should, too! Stand mixers are a kitchen staple and countertop piece. I use mine for mixing cookie and cake batters, bread and loaf batters, for whipping frosting and coconut whipped cream, combining piecrust and other doughs—you name it, I mix it. A stand mixer is certainly an investment, so my advice is to get a good one and get the color you want, because that mixer is going to stay on your counter . . . maybe forever!

CHEF'S KNIFE: This sounds like a no-brainer, but I am shocked how many people don't have a chef's knife in their kitchen! It is essential and, like a stand mixer, a good-quality one is certainly an investment. A chef's knife enables you to cut any shape or size, and is easy to handle. My preferred chef's knife has a six-inch Japanese blade, specifically Shun. Why? The Japanese culture has been handcrafting steel blades for centuries—they know what they're doing. Japanese chef's knives have a layered steel blade, which makes for a more precise and sharper cut, plus the handle and weight of the blade itself are very light, so the overall weight of the knife is much less than a knife with a German blade, for instance. And for someone who's a weakling like me, it's absolutely perfect. Trust me on this!

VEGETABLE PEELER: This sounds standard, but not only do I use my vegetable peeler to peel veggies and the rough outer layers on root vegetables, but I make vegetable ribbons from carrots and zucchini and citrus peels with it as well. This is a perfect tool to use for my Vietnamese-Style Vermicelli Noodle Salad on page 108, to make vegetable ribbons as a shortcut to julienning the vegetables by hand.

NONSTICK SKILLETS: Another obvious, but underrated, kitchen tool. You'll notice that a lot, if not all, of my recipes in this book are cooked in a nonstick skillet. My advice is to invest in a set of three aluminum, good-quality nonstick skillets (small, medium, and large), preferably dishwasher-safe with a steel handle. I find these pans distribute heat evenly while cooking, are easy to clean up, and are oven-safe and lightweight.

STAINLESS-STEEL THREE-QUART SAUCEPAN: Yet another obvious but overlooked kitchen tool; I love my steel saucepan. I use it to boil pasta and make savory sauces (and gooey vegan caramel sauce), syrups, glazes—the list goes on and on! I find this size and style of pot very versatile, especially since we are not cooking for a large crowd with these recipes.

CAST-IRON AEBLESKIVER PAN: This one is a *weird* but essential pan for my Corn Bread Gulab Jamuns on page 82. Known as a Danish pancake pan, or in my family's household, "the fud pan," as we use it to make fud—a rice and lentil fermented dough, mixed with tempered spices, and cooked until golden brown and crisp and served with spicy coconut chutney. Sounds delicious, right? It is. I love this pan—it's fun, different, and alleviates the need for deep-frying my gulab jamuns. Invest in a heavyweight, cast-iron aebleskiver pan. Like other cast-iron pans, it will last forever!

LOAF PAN: A standard nonstick 8½ x 4½ x 2½-inch loaf pan is great to bake loaf cakes, breads, savory dishes like a potato gratin, and most importantly, to bake up my Almond-Tahini Cake with Rose Syrup and Pistachio on page 179.

BUNDT CAKE PAN: I absolutely love this pan—you add regular ol' cake batter, and it turns into something whimsical. I especially love a miniature Bundt cake pan, which is key for my Bondi Blue Tea Cakes on page 161—the perfectly precious size!

SILICONE SPATULA: Another underrated tool. I not only love the spatula for baking and incorporating batters together, but I use it for cooking savory dishes in my nonstick skillets. It doesn't scratch or stick on the skillet and is perfect for delicate batters (especially when cooking with egg substitutes in a pan) or doing a quick sauté. It is also perfect for making sure you scoop out every last drop of goodness from your food processor or blender!

OFFSET SPATULA: An essential tool for a baker, this is perfect for spreading frosting evenly, distributing batter, carving around a baked cake or loaf pan before unmolding—the uses are endless!

THIN STEEL SPATULA: This tool is great for removing freshly baked cookies, molding piecrust or any dough before baking, and flipping pancakes like my Savory Chickpea Flour Pancakes with Tempered Spices on page 50!

MANDOLINE: This makes slicing and julienning so easy. When used properly with a guard, it can make the work so fast. I have it on hand to thinly slice potatoes, ginger, and even garlic!

PARCHMENT PAPER: Not a tool in the traditional sense, but this is environmentally friendly, nonstick, and has a variety of uses. I use it to line baking sheets and pans, to roll out piecrust, and to line a platter with paper towel to drain excess oil from anything that has been shallow-fried.

ALL ABOUT SPICES!

I feel like there is a misconception around dried spices. Granted, they are not fresh vegetables or fruits, but that doesn't mean they can't lose their freshness, taste, and aroma. I treat spices similarly to fresh produce, by consistently replenishing them, because they can get stale and lose their flavor. I store them carefully, and I work with them in a specific manner, too. Here are my tips to get the most life and spice (see what I did there?) out of your dried spices.

STORE IN A DARK COOL PLACE: I generally store my dried spices in a dark drawer or cabinet—there should be no direct sunlight or heat consistently hitting the area.

BEST TYPES OF CONTAINERS: I recommend using a steel container—preferably a traditional masala dabba, which is a stainless-steel tin filled with smaller stainless-steel tins—to store your spices. Steel does not absorb any of the fragrance or aroma from the spices and allows them to retain their integrity. The next best choice is glass jars, preferably with an airtight seal, to seal in all the spicy goodness. My last recommendation is recycled plastic containers—I'm sure we all have a ton of takeout plastic containers sitting around, so use them to store spices! Most have an airtight seal and work well to retain the flavor and aroma of the spices. The only problem with plastic (aside from being plastic) is that the container itself will pick up the flavors of the spices (especially strong ones), which will make it unsuitable for future uses.

REFRIGERATE: Some spice blends and seasoning (like masalas) need to be stored in the fridge to retain optimal freshness. For instance, the Dry Peanut Chutney on page 153 is best kept in the fridge, as anything nut-based contains a lot of oil and moisture. So, the key here is if it has an ounce of moisture, it should be kept in the fridge.

SPICE SUBSTITUTIONS

There is an abundance of chilies and spices across the globe, and as much as we want everything available at our fingertips, it's sadly not! To help, I've created some substitutions that you can easily swap in for ingredients throughout this cookbook.

INDIAN GREEN CHILIES: Green arbol or serrano chili peppers have a similar color, texture, and flavor profile.

DRIED RED CHILIES: I use dried Indian red chilies, which pack a punch of spice. If you can't find these at an Indian grocery store or online, use dried cayenne chilies or dried chili de arbol peppers.

RED CHILI POWDER: There are two kinds of red chili powder I refer to throughout my recipes: Indian red chili powder and Kashmiri red chili powder. Indian red chili powder is spicy and vibrant; it can be bought in bulk packages online or at an Indian grocery store and is simply called "red chili powder." An optimal substitute is cayenne pepper. Kashmiri red chili powder is much more vibrant in color but not as spicy as Indian red chili powder. An optimal substitute is paprika mixed with cayenne pepper.

DRIED PEQUIN CHILI PEPPERS: These are small powerhouses—think Chihuahua small—they may look unsuspecting but will attack and bite with all their force and might! Indigenous to Mexico, these are much spicier than jalapeños on the Scoville scale. But the flavor is so delicious—citrusy, smoky, and slightly nutty. These are readily available in supermarkets in the dried spice section. If you have trouble finding them, substitute a dried cayenne pepper—one to two peppers for the Poblano Torta on page 134 is perfect!

FRESH CORIANDER/CILANTRO: Coriander, or cilantro as North and Latin Americans refer to it, has such a distinct flavor and aroma, especially within Indian and Asian cuisines. And because it plays a critical role, there is no great substitute for it. No, flat-leaf parsley is not a substitute in any way—it has a completely different flavor profile (much more floral and less earthy) and does not mesh with Asian flavors well. Fresh cilantro is readily available at grocery stores. If you're one of those folks who don't like the taste, I encourage you to give it a try in these recipes, as it is incorporated in a way that is far different from what you may be used to!

TEMPERING SPICES

A lot of Indian cooking, including the recipes in this cookbook, calls for "tempering spices." So, let's take a minute to actually define that. In Kannada, *wahgarni* means to flash-fry, or temper, spices. There is a technique to this method and I'm going to let you in on my secret, which of course I learned from Maa and then perfected on my own.

FAT: You always want to start with a neutral oil that has a high smoking point—vegetable or canola oil works perfectly. Do not use olive oil or butter, as these forms of oil have a low smoking point and a strong flavor, which may mask and not mesh with the flavor of the spices.

PAN: If possible, try to use a cast-iron or nonstick skillet when tempering spices—basically any vessel that will retain heat well.

TEMPERATURE: You always want to start your pan over medium-high heat. Why not high? Because we don't want the pan to smoke and the oil to burn. Don't add the oil to the pan until the pan becomes hot. Once the oil is hot, either remove the pan from the stove and hold it over the sink (as the spices may splatter when added to the hot oil) or slightly lower the heat. Add the spices and mix constantly until the popping subsides. Once the popping or splattering subsides, immediately remove from the heat and add the spices to your dish—the key is to add the spices when they're still hot to retain the most flavor.

SPICES: Technically, anything can be tempered. Usually, we temper whole dried spices or dried chilies in these recipes, but even fresh items are fabulous when tempered, such as fresh green chilies, fresh curry leaves, and sliced fresh coconut. Tempering these items heightens the flavors without dissipating them completely when mixed with other ingredients.

Now, you should all be experts in tempering spices!

COOKING WITH WHOLE SPICES

You'll notice throughout my cookbook that I mostly use whole spices. Why? Well, as mentioned in the Storing Spices section (see page 15), whole spices pack a punch of flavor, contain natural oils, and a little goes a long way. Once spices are ground, they immediately start losing their flavor and can become stale quickly (kind of like an expensive car leaving the dealership). It is common practice to cook with whole spices within many regional Indian cooking styles. And I personally love getting a pop of flavor in each bite when I'm eating!

The key to cooking with whole spices is to approach it as you would when tempering the spices (see page 18). You never want to add whole spices to cold oil in a pan—the pan and the oil should be hot. This allows for the maximum flavor and aroma to be released from the spices into the dish. Whole spices can also be ground into a chutney or sauce without having to be toasted—they add a punchy and earthy flavor. If lightly toasted, the oils will release and create a smokier flavor, which is also lovely!

Finally, whole spices give you the flexibility of grinding to a powder if necessary, using a mortar and pestle, of course. So, I hope *The Modern Tiffin* broadens your horizon in cooking with whole spices more than ground—don't be scared, it's delicious!

STORAGE & PREP ADVICE

STORING ROOT VEGETABLES

Root vegetables are any vegetables that need to be pulled out of the ground, such as potatoes, ginger, garlic, beets, and carrots, and should be stored in a cool and dry place. It may not be necessary to store them in the fridge if you live in a cooler climate; I prefer keeping root vegetables in a dark and cool pantry. We don't want direct sunlight hitting the root vegetables because that will cut their life spans short as well as cause them to sprout. The key is to keep the outer peel on the vegetables. Once the peel is removed and the flesh is exposed, the oxygen exposure will drastically reduce the life span. If peeled, store your root veggies in an airtight container in the fridge and use within two to three days. If meal prepping, peel, cut, and soak the vegetables in water with ½ teaspoon lemon juice so they don't oxidize. Young root vegetables with the peel on also store well in the freezer, which I do all the time with fresh ginger! The key is to remove from the freezer at least three hours before cooking to defrost naturally, to alleviate an excess of water in your dish while cooking.

GRATING & STORING FRESH COCONUT

If you decide to take the adventurous route and break, grate, and store your own fresh coconut (see page 12), I recommend storing it in a resealable bag or airtight container in the freezer until ready to use. I think coconut freezes the best out of any produce—the fatty oil protects the coconut from getting freezer burn, and once defrosted, the texture is retained. There are many great-quality shredded coconut brands available in Indian, South Asian, and Chinese markets. Just look in the freezer aisle!

PEELING GINGER

You may have heard of this method already, but the absolute best way to peel ginger is by using a spoon, specifically a thin teaspoon. This delicately removes the peels without tearing off the flesh. Not only is this sustainable, but it's economically efficient. You'll ultimately get more bang for your buck by retaining and cooking with all the ginger flesh! If in a hurry, then the next best option is using a thin paring knife to carefully peel away the ginger skin. If in a further hurry, the ginger can be scrubbed clean, dried off, and chopped with the skin and cooked—this works well with younger ginger, as the skin can be supple enough to consume. No harm, no foul!

WASHING & STORING FRESH HERBS

A trick I learned from my mom (there are many, but this is one in particular that has become so incredibly useful) is properly washing fresh herbs. If you buy fresh herbs in bulk, especially from an Indian or South Asian supermarket, you'll notice that they come with a lot of dry dirt, especially fresh coriander/cilantro. Fresh herbs should not be misted (as they are in American grocery stores) because they are delicate, have a short life span, and adding water just increases their chance of oxidizing and spoiling. Here is what has worked for us, and I recommend you do it as soon as you bring the herbs home.

RINSE AND SOAK: Trim off just the tip of the stem, place into a large bowl, and rinse under cold water by filling the bowl up with water to the rim and then pouring it out while holding the herbs back. Repeat three times until the water starts to run mostly clear. Then cover the herbs with water and let sit for about five minutes—gravity will cause any remaining dirt in the fresh herbs to fall to the bottom of the bowl. Carefully lift the herbs out of the water and give them one last rinse.

DRY: Lay the washed herbs across paper towels to dry completely. This step is key—if you immediately pop these into the fridge, they will turn into spoiled mush with all that moisture! Make sure to separate the herb strands so everything dries.

STORE: Once dried, lightly wrap with a dry paper towel or newspaper, place in an airtight container or resealable bag, and store in the fridge for up to one week.

When cooking with herbs on a daily basis, this prep is key to gain the most out of them and to reduce your cooking and prep time!

VEGAN SUBSTITUTIONS FOR DAIRY & EGGS

We are lucky to live in a world where we have an abundance of plant-based substitutes. Some of the most difficult ingredients to substitute historically have been dairy and eggs. Dairy and eggs are almost essential in most baked goods, sauces, chutneys, and many-a-times drinks. So, here are some of my favorite vegan substitutes.

YOGURTS AND MILKS: Coconut/almond/cashew/oat yogurt; coconut/ oat/almond milk; to make vegan buttermilk, mix 1 cup coconut milk plus 1 tablespoon fresh lemon juice and let sit for 10 to 15 minutes, until the mixture curdles.

CHEESES: Vegan feta cheese replaces cotija cheese (my favorite brands include Violife and Esti); combine 2 tablespoons ground almonds with ¼ to ½ teaspoon kosher salt for Parmesan cheese; vegan mozzarella, pepper jack, and cheddar shreds are readily available (my favorite brands include Field Roast and Miyoko's), as are American, mozzarella, and Gouda vegan slices (my favorite brands include Field Roast and Follow Your Heart).

1 LARGE EGG: 1 tablespoon ground flaxseeds plus 3 tablespoons water; 1 tablespoon ground or whole chia seeds plus 3 tablespoons water; ¼ cup nondairy yogurt; 3 tablespoons egg substitute like Eat Just.

BEST OILS FOR COOKING BY CUISINE TYPE

The type of oil you use to cook with can make or break a dish—I'm not trying to sound dramatic, but it's that important. Every type of oil has its own aroma, flavor, and smoking point. Below, I've outlined the preferred oils to use by chapter:

	VEGETABLE OIL	CANOLA OIL	PEANUT OIL	TOASTED SESAME OIL	COCONUT OIL	EXTRA-VIRGIN OLIVE OIL
Maharashtrian	●	●				
South Indian	●	●			●	
Italian		●				●
Indo-Chinese	●	●	●	●		
American	●	●				
Mexican	●	●				●
Middle Eastern	●	●				●
South Asian	●	●	●	●	●	
Spanish		●				●
Australian	●	●	●			●

(RED indicates the oil has a high smoking point)

HOW TO MAKE ANYTHING PORTABLE

Everything in this cookbook is portable. In reality, most dishes can be made portable. The key is to understand the dish, each component, and how to segment them. For instance, in my Spanish Tiffin, it may seem like the Pan con Spicy Tomate cannot transport well, but understanding that the tomate mixture can be packed separate from the toasted baguette is key to ensure the taste, integrity, and yumminess of the dish upon arrival to your destination. At the end of each recipe, I outline tips for how to make it portable, so there is no excuse! You can have something delicious, healthy, vegan, and global to eat anywhere you go. Just think about all the time, money, and food you'll save by getting into the habit of packing your meals!

MINIMIZING FOOD WASTE

Did you know that eighty billion pounds of food is wasted every year in the United States alone? And nearly 40 percent of the food supply is wasted every year in the United States? I wish I were lying, but I'm not. These statistics are based on a 2020 analysis conducted by RTS (Recycle Track Systems, based in New York City). That is why I treat my food like it's Hindu—there is more than one life, it's stuck in the cycle of Samsara, and it can be reincarnated into all kinds of dishes. I've developed clever ways of repurposing leftovers, incorporating scraps, and repurposing what was once edible into a skincare product. With a little creativity and effort, we can help sustain our planet. So why not start now? Here's a list to get started.

RICE: We often get a ton of rice with our Indian or Asian takeout meals, but instead of chucking that in the garbage, give it a new life! Think of rice as a binder—cooked rice is starchy and can be added to nearly any dish to thicken it up. You can add it to cooked beans and veggies to make a wholesome veggie burger; or use it to create a delicious homemade arancini (rice ball); or sauté that rice up with some spices, veggies, and garam masala to make a stovetop biryani. The point here is that rice can help create or elevate a dish and be given a new life. There are a few recipes in this cookbook that call for leftover rice, so I hope you get a chance to explore them and expand your starchy horizon!

PASTA: I absolutely love working with leftover pasta—there are so many great things you can do. One of my favorite dishes to make is a pasta "pizza"—toss your leftover pasta with some additional sauce of your liking, add in some vegan mozzarella shreds, and cook it on the stove for five minutes. Then transfer to the oven to finish it off. Once crisp, cut it in slices, and you have yourself a pasta pizza! Another fun way to use leftover pasta is in soup. Ever heard of minestrone? It usually has pasta shells, so all you have to do is chop up your leftover pasta, place it into a bubbling vegetable broth with veggies of choice and some spices, and you're good to go! How fun is that?

VEGETABLE SCRAPS: One of the most wasted food items in the United States is produce—a lot of produce doesn't even make it to grocery shelves, and the produce that does is tossed in the garbage if not bought in time. For instance, we (as a society) are in the habit of using only the cauliflower florets and not the leaves. But the leaves are perfectly edible and absolutely delicious. I use vegetable scraps in a few of my recipes in this cookbook, and I think they need to be given a chance. So instead of throwing those leaves away, sauté them with your cauliflower! A fantastic way to use up root vegetable peels and other vegetable scraps is to make a broth—cover the scraps with water and bring to a boil, then simmer until all of the scraps have softened and broken down. Strain and store the broth in an airtight container or jar for up to a week. And if all else fails, compost your scraps—at your local compost bins, farmers' market, or even in your own backyard. How do you think fertilizer is made for new crops to grow?

SKINCARE: No, I'm not here to tell you about my skincare routine, but rather that you can even use food scraps to create DIY, at-home, all-natural vegan skincare products! Are you in the habit of making coffee with fresh grounds? A great way to repurpose those grounds is into a body scrub—once the grounds have been used, place them onto a paper towel–lined plate and let dry. Once dry, store the grounds in an airtight container in a cool and dry place, ensuring that no moisture enters. Once you've accumulated about ½ cup of grounds, mix with 1 tablespoon coconut oil (which is naturally antibacterial) and 1 tablespoon raw cane sugar. This scrub can be used all over your body to buff, shine, and remove dead skin cells. Store it in the fridge for up to 1 month. How cool is that?

ONE

The MAHARASHTRIAN

❦

TIFFIN

Modern Shaboodani

32

Indian Home Fries with Peanuts

35

Cucumber-Carrot Raita

37

Spicy Chickpea Bhel Puri

38

Coconut Masala-Stuffed Okra

40

India is regional—maybe you've heard that before, maybe you haven't. But take it from someone who is not among the majority of her ethnic group in America—India is very regionalized. A large majority of Indians in the Western world, aka America, are from Punjab, Gujarat, and South India, which is ultimately reflected in the food available at "Indian" restaurants. Let me break this down for you: most restaurants that serve "Indian food" are often referring to North Indian (Punjabi) food, which has a heavy British influence (from the era of British colonization in India)—so that's your garlic naan, chicken tikka masala, and daal makhani, for example. In some cases it's referring to Gujarati food—a thali, which is a large plate with several vegetarian dishes and roti. And in some cases it's South Indian food—dosa (cue dosa man in Washington Square Park, Manhattan), idli, sambar, and chutney.

But why am I talking about all of this? Well, there is one style of regional Indian cuisine that is rarely (and in most cases, never) offered at restaurants, and that is Maharashtrian food. And if you guessed that I'm Maharashtrian, you guessed right! I am Maharashtrian, which means my family is from the state of Maharashtra, specifically Mumbai and the surrounding Maharashtra/ Karnataka bordering areas, Belgaum and Ankali. The type of food my family and I ate growing up at home on Staten Island, New York, was not available in restaurants, and probably will not be for the foreseeable future. And to be honest, I'm okay with that! The lack of availability makes Maharashtrian food feel much more special and homey to me.

So, for my first chapter, I want to open up my home to you with a few of my original renditions of classic dishes that I ate growing up and still eat today. You bet I'm going home and bothering Maa to make me everything, even now!

Maharashtrian food tends to be on the lighter side—most of the dishes are sautéed, without any gravies, are vegetable forward, full of texture, and of course, spicy! I hope these dishes make it into your weekly repertoire of go-to recipes. And remember, India is regionalized, which means there are hundreds, if not thousands, of dishes to try. So, step aside garlic naan and chicken tikka masala, because we have a new girl in town and she's spicy!

Modern Shaboodani

⇒) SERVES 2 (⇐

When you grow up in a Hindu household, there are a lot of traditions and customs that are not only rooted in the culture, but in the religion. To put it simply, there are a lot of events that occur on a weekly or even daily basis that are aligned in purposeful Hindu traditions. One of those traditions is fasting. Every Saturday of my childhood my family and I fasted, in showing our respect to Lord Shiva, and my father is a particular observer of this fast. But this wasn't a typical fast where you don't eat the whole day and then eat whatever you'd like in the evening. The fast was observed for the first half of the day, and we broke our fast with a specific dish called shaboodani, which was a recipe of white pearl tapioca made with cumin, chilies, peanuts, potatoes, and coconut. Garlic and onion are meant to be avoided during this meal—this practice of avoiding root vegetables is very common among folks following Jainism, which is a derivative of Hinduism.

This dish is filled with complex carbs, healthy fats, and protein and sustains you throughout the day. Not to mention, it is absolutely delicious. It's such an interesting combination of textures—it's basically like eating a dish made out of tiny spicy "bobas," crunchy peanuts, soft potatoes, and sweet coconut. However, traditional shaboodani is a bit labor-intensive. First, you have to source good-quality dry white tapioca. Then it has to be soaked for a minimum of three to four hours in water and then cooked. My modern-day life has no time for that! But this is one of my favorite dishes to eat on the weekends, so I wanted to recreate shaboodani into a "Modern Shaboodani," which has all the same great flavors and textural elements but is made with pearl couscous! Now you can bring a bit of my family tradition into your home.

- 1 tablespoon plus 1 teaspoon coconut oil or neutral oil
- 1 cup pearl couscous
- Heaping ¼ teaspoon cumin seeds
- 5 to 6 curry leaves (optional)
- 3 Indian green chilies, minced, seeds and all! (see Note)
- 1 teaspoon kosher salt, or to taste
- ¼ cup plus 1 tablespoon unsalted dry-roasted ground peanuts
- ½ teaspoon raw cane sugar
- ½ cup grated fresh coconut
- ¼ wedge fresh lemon
- ½ cup coarsely chopped fresh cilantro (stems and all!)

PREPARE THE COUSCOUS: In a small pot, place 1¼ cups water over medium heat to bring to a boil. Once the water is boiling, add the 1 teaspoon oil and the couscous. Stir to make sure all of the couscous is covered and incorporated into the water. Reduce the heat to low, just until the mixture is simmering. Cover and cook for 8 to 10 minutes, until the water is absorbed and the couscous is soft and cooked through. Drain the couscous in a sieve to remove any excess moisture. Tip: if the couscous is sticking together, spray with some cooking spray and mix.

TEMPER THE SPICES: In a large nonstick skillet, heat the 1 tablespoon oil over high heat. Once the oil is hot (you will see ripples in the oil), add the cumin seeds. They will pop for about 15 seconds. Once the popping subsides, lift your skillet away from the stove into the sink (if it's nearby), add the curry leaves, if using, and stand back. These leaves will aggressively pop and splash oil, so be careful! Place the skillet back on the stove once the popping subsides and reduce the heat to medium. Add the chilies and sauté for 1 minute.

MAKE THE SHABOODANI: Once your couscous is cooked and drained of excess water, add it to your tempered spices and toss to coat thoroughly. At this point, add the salt, the ¼ cup of the ground peanuts, and the sugar. Toss and cook for 1 to 2 minutes—we want all the flavors to seep into the couscous. Give it a taste; the flavor should be spicy, nutty, and savory. Adjust the salt accordingly.

NOW TIME FOR THE COCONUT: Add about three-quarters of the coconut, reserving the rest for garnish. Toss to incorporate thoroughly. Next, give the shaboodani a squeeze of lemon juice from the wedge and toss in three-quarters of the cilantro, reserving the remainder for garnish. Before serving, give it another taste and adjust for salt if necessary. The coconut balances the sweetness, the lemon adds the fresh punch of citrusy flavor, and the cilantro adds freshness.

PLACE THE SHABOODANI INTO ONE of your tiffin sections and garnish with the remaining coconut, the 1 tablespoon peanuts, and the cilantro. This tastes amazing when served warm, but is absolutely delicious eaten at room temperature if you take your tiffin on the go!

✕ ─────────────────────────────

NOTE: Green arbol chili peppers or serrano chili peppers can be substituted for Indian green chilies.

Indian Home Fries with Peanuts

SERVES 2

Who doesn't like home fries? I dare you to find someone who openly admits that they don't like home fries, or even potatoes for that matter. And if they do admit it, I'm convinced they're an alien! Now, getting back to earth—we made these Indian Home Fries with Peanuts to accompany our Modern Shaboodani on Saturdays, but honestly, these are so great on their own. They have so much flavor, these Indian Home Fries with Peanuts can easily be treated like the independent women they are! Sweet, crunchy, spicy—everything you need in a well-balanced dish. They're perfect as an accompaniment to your savory brunch, sweet pancakes, or even as a warm salad. Plus, this is perfect to make with a variety of potatoes. Don't have sweet potatoes on hand? No worries, russets work just fine. And even fingerlings are a great choice! Clearly, I'm a potato enthusiast and don't discriminate. Fun fact: I cooked up a rendition of these Indian Home Fries with Peanuts on Food Network's *Cooks vs. Cons* in 2017 and I won! So, to answer your question, yes, this recipe is a showstopping, award-winning, sassy little independent thang!

- 1 tablespoon coconut oil or neutral oil
- Heaping ¼ teaspoon cumin seeds
- 2 medium sweet potatoes, peeled and cut into ⅛-inch-thick slices
- 2 Indian green chilies, cut in half lengthwise (see Note)
- 3 tablespoons unsalted dry-roasted peanuts
- 3 to 4 tablespoons coarsely chopped fresh cilantro (stems and all!)
- 1 teaspoon kosher salt
- ¼ wedge fresh lemon

Method follows

TEMPER THE SPICES: In a large nonstick skillet, pour the oil to coat the skillet and place over medium-high heat. Once hot, add the cumin seeds and cook for 30 seconds or so. They will become fragrant and pop.

NEXT, ADD THE POTATOES AND TOSS with the cumin seeds. After about 60 seconds, add the chilies, 2 tablespoons of the peanuts, and 2 tablespoons of the cilantro. Make sure to spread the potatoes in the skillet so each touches the pan to evenly cook. Add the salt, making sure to sprinkle it all over the potatoes.

COOK FOR ABOUT 15 MINUTES, until the potatoes are cooked through, flipping halfway through and browned on each side—like home fries! Do not cover at any point, otherwise the potatoes will steam and not char. Right at the end, squeeze in the lemon juice from the wedge, add the remaining 1 to 2 tablespoons of cilantro depending on your taste, and toss. Garnish with the remaining 1 tablespoon peanuts. This tastes great served warm, but is absolutely delicious eaten at room temperature (which I prefer) if you take your tiffin on the go! It pairs perfectly with the Modern Shaboodani, over rice, or even on its own!

NOTE: Green arbol chili peppers or serrano chili peppers can be substituted for Indian green chilies.

Cucumber-Carrot Raita

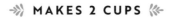

MAKES 2 CUPS

Indian food in general is all about balance—balance of flavors, textures, and dishes. And because Maharashtrian food tends to be spicy, we like to accompany it with something cool and refreshing so we can . . . well . . . keep eating! I love raita—it's super refreshing and complementary to most dishes without overpowering the flavors with its creaminess. And this Cucumber-Carrot Raita is the perfect balance of tart, sweet, and delicately creamy from the coconut yogurt. So, you don't feel like you're eating a whole pot of cream. I love eating this as a side to my Modern Shaboodani and Indian Home Fries with Peanuts, or spread on a sandwich, or even just accompanying plain rice.

1 cup unsweetened plain coconut yogurt

¼ cup plain nondairy sour cream

½ medium English cucumber, peeled and shredded

1 small orange carrot, peeled and shredded

⅛ teaspoon cumin seeds

Pinch of kosher salt, plus more for seasoning

Pinch of freshly ground black pepper

¼ teaspoon fresh lemon zest

¼ teaspoon raw cane sugar, plus more for seasoning

3 tablespoons coarsely chopped fresh cilantro (stems and all!)

IN A MEDIUM BOWL, whisk together the coconut yogurt and sour cream until smooth with no visible lumps. Add in the shredded cucumber and carrots—notice we did not soak out the vegetables' moisture, as we want the moisture to incorporate into the mixture for a smooth raita. Stir with a spoon until completely combined.

USING A MORTAR AND PESTLE, grind the cumin seeds until fine and fragrant.

SPICE IT UP: Add the ground cumin, salt, pepper, lemon zest, and sugar and mix with a spoon to combine well. At this point, we want to give it a taste—if it is too tart, add in a bit more sugar. If it tastes a bit too bland, add a bit more salt. Lastly, add 2 tablespoons of the cilantro and mix.

GARNISH with the remaining 1 tablespoon cilantro and serve! This combines perfectly well with the Modern Shaboodani and Indian Home Fries. If traveling with your tiffin, place a small ice pack in your bag, or my trick is to place a few ice cubes directly in the raita when packed in your tiffin. That way it will be at room temperature by the time you reach your destination!

Spicy Chickpea Bhel Puri

 SERVES 2

I'm going to let you in on a little secret—I am a junk food connoisseur. I'm not talking about your typical chips and Ding Dongs, I'm talking about spicy, crunchy, mouthwatering Mumbai street food. Yup! I love street food so much that whenever I land at Chhatrapati Shivaji Maharaj International Airport in Mumbai (and I grew up visiting every year of my life, even into my adult years), I make my cousins stop at the late-night pav bhaji stand on the way to my family's home. I order a plate of piping hot pav bhaji—a vegetarian "sloppy joe" with fresh Indian bread that's been toasted to perfection—and promptly stuff my face. This isn't your typical fast food; it's Indian street food and it's full of spices, texture, and veggies. So technically, it's good for you!

Now, enough about pav bhaji. Let's talk about another one of my street-food favorites: bhel puri. The classic bhel puri is made with thin sev, or "crunchies" that are Indian crisps made of all-purpose flour and sometimes besan (chickpea flour), tossed together with boiled chopped potatoes, fresh chopped tomato, spicy green chilies, fresh cilantro, and sweet tamarind chutney and spicy green chutney. And it's typically served in a newspaper cone. Simply the best. I remember next to my auntie and uncle's flat in Nariman's Point, Mumbai, where we normally stayed while visiting, there was a bhel wallah standing with his cart right by the apartment building's parking garage, with all the bhel fixins', just whipping up bhel in the fastest way you've ever seen. It was mesmerizing, but more importantly, it made me hungry for bhel. And it was the best.

My Spicy Chickpea Bhel Puri is a recreation of one of my favorite Mumbai street food dishes, and it brings me straight back to the motherland. Crunchy, spicy, tangy, salty—everything you can ask for in a junk-food dish!

1 (15-ounce) can low-sodium chickpeas (see Notes)

1 tablespoon neutral oil

½ teaspoon red chili powder (see Notes)

¼ teaspoon amchur (mango) powder

½ teaspoon kosher salt, plus more for seasoning

¼ teaspoon freshly ground black pepper

½ large beefsteak tomato, seeds removed, diced small

2 Indian green chilies, minced, seeds and all! (see Notes)

1 scallion, sliced

¼ cup coarsely chopped fresh cilantro (stems and all!), plus more for seasoning

3 tablespoons tamarind chutney (see Notes)

Hefty pinch of chaat masala, plus more for seasoning (optional)

Thin sev, for garnish (optional)

PREP THE CHICKPEAS: Drain the chickpeas (reserving the chickpea water for another use) and rinse and thoroughly dry them. Lay the chickpeas on a paper towel to absorb the moisture and let air-dry for a minimum of 30 minutes. While they're drying, remove as many chickpea skins as you can. Set them aside for another use.

LET'S GET TOASTY: Preheat the oven to 400°F and line a large cookie sheet with parchment paper. Transfer the dried chickpeas to a large bowl and add the oil, red chili powder, amchur powder, salt, and pepper. Toss until thoroughly coated. Lay the chickpeas out in a single layer on the cookie sheet. Bake for about 15 minutes, until the chickpeas are crispy and start slightly splitting. Remove and let cool completely.

BHEL TIME: Wipe down the same large bowl used to toss the chickpeas. Add the cooled chickpeas, tomatoes, green chilies, scallion, and cilantro. Toss to combine. Next, add the tamarind chutney and chaat masala, if using. Toss to incorporate thoroughly. Taste and add more chaat masala if it needs more salt. If you're not using chaat masala, add a pinch of salt.

SERVE AND GARNISH with a handful of thin sev, if using. If not, garnish with some extra cilantro. If traveling, do not garnish with the thin sev—bring that separately and garnish right before eating or the sev will become soggy and unpleasant. I use a resealable bag to pack my sev.

✂ ————————————————

NOTES: When you open a can of chickpeas, chances are you're going to drain and rinse them, which means you're tossing that liquid gold down the drain. Instead of doing that, drain the chickpeas into a bowl and reserve the liquid. For best results, place it in a steel or glass bowl and refrigerate until cold, for up to 2 days. Using a simple hand mixer, whisk, or stand mixer fitted with a whisk attachment, whip the chickpea liquid into a meringue-like texture and fold into chocolate to create a rich and fluffy chocolate mousse, make into actual meringues, or bake into bread, and so much more. And this is why I refer to it as liquid gold.

Green arbol chili peppers or serrano chili peppers can be substituted for Indian green chilies. Red chili powders vary in heat and color. Using an Indian red chili powder, found in an Indian grocery store or online, is best for this dish.

See the Glossary (page 194) on buying the best store-bought chutneys and some of my favorite brands.

Coconut Masala-Stuffed Okra

⇒ SERVES 2 ⇐

Let me guess—you don't like okra. Am I right? I truly believe that when a person doesn't like a vegetable or specific ingredient, they just haven't tasted it cooked the right way! I happen to be not among the norm (honestly, there isn't that much that is "normal" about me) and I absolutely love okra. It's my favorite vegetable. I love the way it looks and tastes, but more importantly, I *love* its versatility. I think I get this from my mom's side of the family. And that is reflected directly in this dish.

My Coconut Masala–Stuffed Okra is a rendition of a family favorite from Ankali, Karnataka (where my mother's side of the family mainly resides), and was specifically a favorite dish of Aai, my maternal grandmother. Her recipe was the best and she passed it on to Maa. These delicate lady fingers are stuffed with a spicy coconut masala mixture and pan-seared to perfection. You will find zero slime here—I assure you! This dish is very special to me. Not only is okra my favorite vegetable, but it connects me back to my Ankali family, our family farms and, in some way, connects me to my Aai, with whom I spent the most time with (in terms of elders) as a child in India. And I guarantee that if you're an okra hater, you will be an okra lover once you try this!

- 8 to 10 fresh okras
- 1½ teaspoons plus ¼ teaspoon coriander seeds
- 1½ teaspoons plus ¼ teaspoon cumin seeds
- 3 dried red chilies
- ½ teaspoon turmeric powder
- 4 tablespoons grated fresh coconut, plus more for garnish
- Pinch of kosher salt
- 1 to 2 teaspoons coconut oil or neutral oil
- ¼ wedge fresh lemon
- 2 tablespoons coarsely chopped fresh cilantro (stems and all!)

PREP THE OKRAS: Using a damp towel, wipe down each of your okras from top to bottom, rather than rinsing them off under water. This prevents them from getting slimy while cooking. Using a paring knife, carefully make a slit lengthwise down the okra, being careful not to slit all the way through. You just want to create an opening. Set aside.

MAKE THE STUFFING: In a small blender or food processor, blend together the 1½ teaspoons coriander seeds, the 1½ teaspoons cumin seeds, 2 of the red chilies, the turmeric, coconut, and salt until finely incorporated. The mixture will be very fragrant and medium brown.

USING A TEASPOON, stuff each cavity of the okra with the coconut masala mixture until completely filled and the stuffing is exposed a bit at the slit. Repeat until all the okras are stuffed. You may have some stuffing left over depending on how large your okras are, and if so, set it aside.

HEAT A MEDIUM NONSTICK SKILLET over medium-high heat. Add the oil and once it's hot, add the ¼ teaspoon coriander seeds and the ¼ teaspoon cumin seeds and break up the remaining red chili. Let temper in the hot oil for 30 seconds until fragrant. Add any leftover stuffing and toss to coat. Now add the stuffed okras, making sure each touches the bottom of the skillet without overcrowding. Reduce the heat to medium-low and cook for about 2 minutes,

uncovered. Cover with a lid and cook for another 2 to 3 minutes, until one side becomes slightly browned. Then, using tongs, flip to cook the other side, covering again. After another 3 to 4 minutes, uncover and check to see if the okras are fork-tender. If not, continue cooking until browned and the okras are tender.

SQUEEZE IN THE LEMON JUICE from the wedge and toss to coat all of the okras. Transfer to a serving dish or your tiffin. Garnish with the cilantro. This tastes delicious at room temperature!

TWO

The
SOUTH INDIAN
TIFFIN

Spice-Rubbed Cauliflower Steaks with Pistachio & Cilantro Gremolata

47

Coconut Yogurt Rice with Tempered Spices (Wahgarni)

49

Savory Chickpea Flour Pancakes (Chuvie) with Tempered Spices (Wahgarni)

50

Red Chili & Mustard Seed Apple Slaw

53

Saffron Sheera with Cardamom & Buttery Golden Cashews

54

I've given you this whole spiel on how I'm Maharashtrian in Chapter 1. And it's all 100 percent true! But what I didn't mention is what language I speak or what my native "tongue" is, and at this point you might be wondering, "What is it, Priyanka?!" Well, it's Kannada and Marathi.

Now you're like, "Kannada, you say? But isn't that a South Indian language?!"

Yes, you're correct! Kannada *is* a South Indian language, but Maharashtra and Karnataka are bordering states on the west coast of India and it is very common for people who are regionally from that area to speak both (and more) languages. However, there is one unique factor as to why my families speak both languages and why Kannada is considered our "mother tongue." We are Lingayat—a specific sect of Hinduism who are Lord Shiva worshippers and followers of Basaveswara, a twelfth-century Kannadiga (aka Kannada speaker from Karnataka) philosopher, educator, and social reformer who created an educational, spiritual, and social community that did not discriminate based on gender, social status, caste, rituals, or anything of the kind. It was open to all. His philosophy and followers created what is known as Lingayatism. The legend goes that when Basaveswara, a devotee of Lord Shiva, passed, he disappeared into the form of "Linga," or an avatar of Lord Shiva.

Big side note here: my family and I speak a hybrid form of Kannada since we're Maharashtrian. It's almost a Kannada-Marathi slang. And another (hilarious) side note: my parents kept Marathi as a secret language between them and only taught my sisters and me Kannada. I am 100 percent serious about this!

"But Priyanka, what does this have to do with food?!"

Understanding my background is key to understanding why I speak Kannada and how my background influences my "South Indian-ness," per se! And a lot of those influences manifest themselves in food. We grew up eating a ton of dishes that were influenced by South Indian cuisine, like dosa, idli, sambar, and chutney, and also the specific style of eating—lots of koshumbris (side salads/condiments), lots of creative rice-based dishes, vegetables galore, coconut, tangy flavors, and lots of tempered spices, or *wahgarni* in Kannada, such as black mustard seeds, red chilies, and curry leaves.

Spice-Rubbed Cauliflower Steaks with Pistachio & Cilantro Gremolata

⇛⇛ SERVES 2 ⇚⇚

I'm going to be honest—there aren't too many South Indian dishes that involve cauliflower. It's mainly used in North Indian dishes like aloo gobi, gobi paratha, and an Indo-Chinese dish called gobi Manchurian. But I love cauliflower and we make a really yummy sautéed cauliflower dish at home that is so simple, yet full of dynamic flavor—florets sautéed with onions, turmeric, our family's red chili masala, black mustard seeds, and fresh cilantro. My Spice-Rubbed Cauliflower Steaks combine a few elements from the dish I grew up eating at home but, of course, with a Priyanka twist. The cauliflower is cooked to perfection and topped with a crunchy gremolata and koshumbri. Normally served as a side complementary to meals, this Tomato Coconut Koshumbri adds the perfect level of freshness and sweetness to our spicy cauliflower steaks. You're going to love it!

CAULIFLOWER STEAKS

- **1 teaspoon coriander seeds**
- **2 dried red chilies**
- **1 teaspoon black peppercorns**
- **¼ teaspoon kosher salt**
- **1 small head cauliflower**
- **1 tablespoon olive oil**
- **1 tablespoon neutral oil, for cooking**
- **1 medium yellow onion, thinly sliced**
- **2 cloves garlic, minced**

PISTACHIO CILANTRO GREMOLATA

- **2 tablespoons unsalted pistachios, coarsely chopped**
- **¼ cup coarsely chopped fresh cilantro (stems and all!)**
- **1 tablespoon good-quality olive oil**
- **¼ teaspoon fresh lemon zest**
- **Pinch of kosher salt**

TOMATO COCONUT KOSHUMBRI

- **1 roma tomato, diced (juice and all)**
- **1 Indian green chili, minced (see Note)**
- **2 tablespoons grated fresh coconut**
- **¼ wedge fresh lemon**
- **Pinch of kosher salt**

Method follows

MAKE THE SPICE BLEND FOR THE CAULIFLOWER: Using a mortar and pestle, coarsely grind together the coriander seeds, red chilies, peppercorns, and the ¼ teaspoon salt. Set aside.

PREPARE THE CAULIFLOWER: Remove the leaves, but do not discard! We will be using them. Trim about ¼ inch of the end of the stem. Set the cauliflower upright on your cutting board, and using a large chef's knife, cut the first steak by cutting into the head about 1 inch. The end pieces may slightly fall apart, which is fine. You should get 2 to 3 fully intact "steaks." Set those steaks flat on the cutting board.

GET RUBBIN': Drizzle the cauliflower steaks with the olive oil all over—front, back, top, and bottom. Using your hands, rub the ground spices all over the steaks, making sure to get into the nooks and crannies of the florets and all over. Rub any remaining spice mixture onto the cauliflower leaves.

GET COOKING: Set a large nonstick pan over medium-high heat. Add the neutral oil and, once hot, add the onion and garlic. Reduce the heat to medium and sauté for 3 to 4 minutes, until the onion becomes translucent and has sweated out its moisture and the garlic is golden. Carefully place each steak into the pan, being sure not to overcrowd. Cook each side for 10 to 15 minutes, until charred and fork-tender. While the steaks cook, add the cauliflower leaves, allowing them to cook alongside the onion. Add any small florets from the cutting board, as well.

MEANWHILE, MAKE THE GREMOLATA AND KOSHUMBRI: In a small bowl, mix all the ingredients for the gremolata and set aside so all the flavors can seep in together. In another small bowl, mix together all the ingredients for the koshumbri, except for the salt. Adding the salt too early will let out all the moisture from the tomatoes and coconut, making the koshumbri too watery. Set aside.

PLATE UP: On a serving platter or in your tiffin, lay down the charred cauliflower leaves and onion mixture first. Then carefully add the cauliflower steaks on top next to each other—if using a small tiffin/portable container, it is okay to break up your cauliflower into bite-size florets. Using a spoon, distribute some of the koshumbri across the cauliflower steaks and sprinkle a tiny pinch of kosher salt across the koshumbri. Finally, top off with the gremolata. A great aspect of this dish is that it actually tastes better when the components have sat together for a length of time, which means that if you're on the go, these will taste even better later!

NOTE: Green arbol chili peppers or serrano chili peppers can be substituted for Indian green chilies.

Coconut Yogurt Rice with Tempered Spices (Wahgarni)

⇒ SERVES 2 ⇐

If I could name a quintessential South Indian dish, it would 100 percent be yogurt rice. There is not a Hindu temple or South Indian household that does not have yogurt rice on the menu. It's a staple! It's a complete balance of carbohydrates, proteins, spices, and most importantly—satisfaction! When we were younger, we went on quite a few road trips—to Lake George, Vermont, Washington, DC, so many places! And I always remember Maa packing a tiffin with one dish being yogurt rice. And I bet we weren't the only Indian family to do that. This dish is easy to make, easy to pack, and travels perfectly.

My Coconut Yogurt Rice with Tempered Spices does that and more! It is 100 percent vegan (obviously), but it goes one step further because it incorporates leftover rice! No food waste in my house, and I strive to extend that to your home, too. This dish tastes better with leftover rice because the starches in the rice become more resistant, which means that flavors will stick to the rice better than to freshly cooked rice. Mind blown, no?

- 1 cup unsweetened plain coconut yogurt
- 1 (½-inch) piece fresh ginger, peeled and grated
- 2 Indian green chilies, or 1 serrano chili pepper, minced
- ¼ teaspoon kosher salt
- Pinch of raw cane sugar
- 1 cup (more or less) leftover cooked basmati rice
- 2 to 3 tablespoons unsweetened plain nondairy creamer
- 2 teaspoons neutral oil
- ½ teaspoon black mustard seeds
- 1 dried red chili
- 1 tablespoon unsalted dry-roasted peanuts
- 4 to 5 curry leaves (optional)

PREPARE THE YOGURT: In a medium bowl, add the coconut yogurt, ginger, green chilies, salt, and a pinch of sugar, and mix. Taste and add more salt if necessary. Add the basmati rice and mix to coat completely. Add 1 tablespoon of the nondairy creamer and mix. The consistency should be similar to a creamy rice pudding, so add more creamer if necessary. Taste again and add more salt if needed.

TEMPER THE SPICES: Place a small skillet over medium-high heat and add the neutral oil. Once the oil is hot, add the mustard seeds, red chili, and peanuts. Reduce the heat to medium and swirl in the oil for 30 seconds until fragrant. Then, if using, add the curry leaves and stand back, as these will pop aggressively! Once the popping subsides, swirl and immediately pour onto the coconut yogurt rice. Stir to incorporate. Serve immediately, or let sit for at least 1 hour for flavors to incorporate further. This dish travels well, as it tastes great at room temperature and the spices help preserve the dish.

Savory Chickpea Flour Pancakes (Chuvie) with Tempered Spices (Wahgarni)

 MAKES 8 THIN PANCAKES

There are dozens—maybe hundreds—of different pancake-style dishes within Indian cooking. I can name at least ten right off the top of my head! And trust me, they never get old. There's something about a pancake in any cuisine that makes it fun to eat, it's delicious, and honestly, I've never met anyone who doesn't like a pancake. And if they say they don't like pancakes, do not trust them. I repeat, do not trust them.

One of the pancakes my mom often made for us on the weekends was tomato chuvie, a chickpea flour–based batter mixed with spices and tomatoes, cooked up until golden and crisp and served with sweet and spicy Indian ketchup. So delicious. My mouth is watering just reminiscing about it. But the problem with a lot of these pancakes is they have to be eaten fresh, otherwise they lose their texture and charm. So, I was determined to create a rendition of chuvie that is easy to make ahead of time, healthy, and obviously delicious! And that's when my Savory Chickpea Flour Pancakes with Tempered Spices (aka Wahgarni) were born! They retain their texture even if made ahead of time, and why healthy? Well, chickpea flour is made from ground dried chickpeas, so it's all protein and very high in potassium. It's a win-win in my book.

1 cup chickpea/besan flour, sifted

1 tablespoon neutral oil, for cooking

½ teaspoon cumin seeds

¼ teaspoon black mustard seeds

1 to 2 dried red chilies

4 to 5 curry leaves (optional)

Pinch of kosher salt

Pinch of freshly ground black pepper

MAKE THE BATTER: Place the chickpea flour in a large bowl and gradually add in about ¾ cup water. Whisk until smooth and lump-free. Add another ¾ cup water and mix—the batter should be fairly thin like a crepe batter, not thick like a traditional pancake batter.

MAKE IT SPICY: To make the tadka, aka tempered spices, place a small nonstick skillet over high heat. Add the oil; once the oil is shimmering and has ripples, it's hot. Bring the skillet over to the sink if nearby, and first add your cumin seeds, black mustard seeds, and red chili (break it in half to reveal the seeds). After 15 seconds, add your curry leaves, if using, and step back, as they will pop aggressively! Once the popping slightly subsides, swirl the skillet around until everything is incorporated, and then pour the spices immediately into the chickpea flour batter. Stir until incorporated. Add the salt and pepper.

COOK 'EM UP: Heat the same skillet over medium heat and use the residual oil to cook the pancakes. Once hot, pour in ¼ cup of the batter and swirl the skillet to spread the batter evenly to coat the skillet. Cook for 3 to 4 minutes, until the sides start looking slightly golden and are bubbling. Flip and cook 3 to 4 minutes on the other side. Both sides should be slightly golden brown and crisp. Remove and repeat until you've cooked all the pancakes. Serve immediately or if traveling, allow the pancakes to cool to room temperature, then place into your tiffin. These pancakes can be eaten hot or at room temperature.

Red Chili & Mustard Seed Apple Slaw

 **SERVES 2**

I've talked about koshumbri a lot in this chapter. One may think I am obsessed, and I am not ashamed of that. How can you not be obsessed with a dish that is *all* about texture and bold flavors, and versatile enough to be paired with anything? If I told you the number of koshumbris my family makes, you might be astonished. We make a koshumbri out of everything—raw mango, tomato, gourds, beets, coconut—you name it, we koshumbri it. However, there is one item I have yet to see a koshumbri for, and that is the classic American apple. So, you know I had to create something that combined both of my worlds, and thus this Red Chili & Mustard Seed Apple Slaw was born. It's a dynamic combination of crunchy and sweet apples with spicy red chilies and bold black mustard seeds. It's a surprisingly awesome combination and I love pairing this with the Savory Chickpea Pancakes from this chapter, or really with any dish in this book!

2 Red Delicious apples

¼ wedge fresh lemon

1 tablespoon coconut oil or neutral oil, for cooking

¼ teaspoon black mustard seeds

2 dried red chilies

Small pinch (less than ⅛ teaspoon) of hing/asafetida (optional)

4 curry leaves (optional)

Pinch of kosher salt

Pinch of freshly ground black pepper

2 tablespoons coarsely chopped fresh cilantro (stems and all!)

1 teaspoon grated fresh coconut

PREP THE APPLES: Using a sharp chef's knife, julienne the apples. You want to do this by first cutting the apple in half, then in half again lengthwise. Once the quarter of the apple is at an angle, carefully use your knife to discard the middle core. Place the palm of your hand on top of the skin side of the apple to cut the apple into thin side rectangles. Once those are cut, you can julienne your rectangles into thin strips. Set the apple strips in a small bowl on the side. Give one small squeeze of the lemon wedge over the apples so they don't oxidize.

TEMPER THE SPICES: Place a small nonstick skillet over medium-high heat. Add the oil and allow it to heat up. Once it is shimmery and you see ripples, it's hot. Lower the heat to medium-low and add the mustard seeds. They will pop, so be careful! Next, break up the red chilies into the skillet and, if using, add the pinch of hing. Lastly, add your curry leaves, if using, and stand back because these pop aggressively! Once the popping subsides, swirl the mixture around until everything is coated, remove from the heat, and immediately pour over the apples and toss. Add the salt and pepper and squeeze the remaining juice from the lemon wedge. Toss and taste, adding more salt if necessary.

GARNISH AND SERVE: Toss in the cilantro and grated coconut right before serving or, if traveling, toss in the coconut and cilantro and place into your tiffin and get goin'; enjoy!

Saffron Sheera with Cardamom & Buttery Golden Cashews

SERVES 2

You thought I would end this chapter without a little dessert action? Come on, you must know by now that Indian sweets are almost diabetically sweet, which means we LOVE our desserts! I will admit, I have a huge sweet tooth (probably larger than my spicy tooth), but I do have a limit as to how sweet I like my desserts. Enter sheera. Sheera, also known as sooji halwa, is made throughout India, and is a balanced dessert usually made of sooji (semolina), nuts, dried fruits, and ghee. And the best part is—it's not diabetically sweet, it's perfect! In Maharashtra and Karnataka, we add a touch of luxury—saffron, cashews, and raisins. Plus, many-a-times we add pineapple, which is my personal favorite. So, my Saffron Sheera with Cardamom & Buttery Golden Cashews is my modern-day rendition of an Indian nationwide classic! Plus, Saffron Sheera is fantastic on-the-go—it tastes just as good the next day and at room temperature.

Fun fact: Sheera is considered an auspicious food, as it is served during many Hindu ceremonies and prayers as an offering to the gods and goddesses, because it includes all the elements that they essentially "require"—nuts, dried fruits, sugar, ghee, and wheat/grain. But clearly, the gods and goddesses have fantastic taste.

- 1 tablespoon plus 1 teaspoon vegan butter
- 1 cup fine semolina (sooji)
- ¼ teaspoon kosher salt
- 1 cup plus 2 tablespoons raw cane sugar
- Pinch of saffron threads
- 1 teaspoon freshly ground cardamom, plus more for garnish
- 2 heaping tablespoons unsalted raw cashews, coarsely chopped
- 1 heaping tablespoon golden raisins

TOAST THE SEMOLINA: In a medium pot, heat the 1 tablespoon vegan butter over medium heat. Once melted, add the semolina, and roast for about 3 minutes, until slightly golden and fragrant.

GET IT BOILING: Add 2½ cups of water and the salt. Stir well and reduce the heat to low. Once the water begins to simmer and reduce, stir in the sugar, saffron threads, and cardamom until well combined. Cover and cook for another 2 to 3 minutes. Once the water is evaporated, it should resemble a thick porridge-like consistency and should be yellow (from the saffron!). Stir until smooth and add a bit more water if it begins to clump together. Give it a taste— it should be very sweet and aromatic. Once the semolina is soft and cooked through, which should be no more than 5 minutes, remove from the heat and let cool.

FINISHING TOUCHES: In a small pan, melt the 1 teaspoon vegan butter over medium-low heat. Add the cashews and raisins and cook for 2 to 3 minutes, until slightly golden.

TO SERVE: Place the Saffron Sheera in serving dishes and top each with the cashew and raisin mixture, plus some cardamom. This tastes best warm, but is also absolutely delicious at room temperature, so, if traveling, place the sheera into your tiffin and garnish with the cashew and raisin mixture. Enjoy at room temperature once you've reached your destination!

THREE

The ITALIAN

TIFFIN

Masala Chickpea Bruschetta

61

Bucatini à la Pumpkin with Pink Peppercorn & Pistachio

63

Cauliflower-Saffron Pasta

66

Indian Stuffed Mushrooms

68

Lemon Risotto with Tempered Spices

70

I know I'm first-generation Indian American, but I may as well be half Italian. When you grow up on Staten Island, sometimes also known as Staten Italy, and you've visited Italy several times over your life, you can pretty much claim you're half Italian, right? I'm sure all the real Italians want to curse me out in some beautiful-sounding Italian words right about now. But food-wise, I'm pretty much half Italian. I can confidently say I grew up eating equal amounts of regional Indian food and Italian food. Aside from the fact that Italian food is literally the *only* type of food available to eat out on Staten Island, it's also really good and comforting. But a distinguishing factor here is that the Italian food that we're privy to in New York (or the States) is Italian American, whereas the food *in* Italy is pretty different. I've been fortunate enough to experience both.

Funny thing about this is, when I think of my first trip to Italy—I was six years old and on a European excursion with my family—there is one experience that I distinctly remember. Unfortunately, it's not the most positive. We toured Florence one whole day and were so tired by the evening. And if you know anything about older European cities, there is a LOT of walking on tiny, cobblestone streets—not something we're used to in the States. And Europeans tend to eat on the later side. So, after already a long day of walking, we walked all the way to a recommended restaurant and the host refused to seat us, because . . . wait for it . . . we were Indian. Yup, this was 1994. We dealt with a lot of discrimination at home, but to experience it more severely while traveling is just a whole other set of emotions. All I could think when I was that age was "Why?" My dad argued with the host— rightfully so, in my opinion—but we ultimately walked away. It didn't make sense. And although that was a weird and hurtful experience, my family and I didn't let it tarnish our experience of the people as a whole, the country, and their food.

I traveled back to Italy as an adult and had a completely different experience. Moral of the story here is—don't let one experience tarnish your image of something, give second chances, and (more importantly) don't let negative people destroy your food experiences. With all that being said, the recipes in this chapter are a culmination of my deep ties to Italian culture on both American and Italian soil. And let me just tell you, it is delicious.

Masala Chickpea Bruschetta

❊ SERVES 2 TO 4 ❊

When I was growing up on Staten Island, or Staten Italy as a lot of us locals like to call it, bruschetta was as frequent on our dinner table as chapati (a thin, delicate Indian bread eaten with vegetables). Traditionally (or as I know it), bruschetta is a toasted slice of Italian bread topped with a tomato-basil-garlic mixture with tons of delicious extra-virgin olive oil. I love bruschetta, but (and completely unrelated to anything I just said) I also love my mom's Maharashtrian Style Chole—a creamy chickpea-based dish with several spices, ginger, garlic, tomatoes, and fresh cilantro. Two completely different dishes, but together they make the marriage that no one saw coming—almost like Priyanka Chopra and Nick Jonas, eh?! This Masala Chickpea Bruschetta is a culmination of my two loves and is perhaps one of my best recipes (dare I say?). It has been my most popular and most requested recipe for the past three years! And the best part is—it's all portable! Pro tip: make all the components ahead of time and assemble right before eating.

YOGURT SAUCE

1 cup unsweetened plain coconut yogurt

½ teaspoon fresh lemon zest

½ teaspoon raw cane sugar

¼ teaspoon kosher salt

½ teaspoon cumin powder

Pinch of freshly ground black pepper

MASALA CHICKPEA TOPPING

½ teaspoon fennel seeds

½ teaspoon coriander seeds

1 tablespoon neutral oil, for cooking

1 small yellow onion, diced

2 cloves garlic, minced

1 (1-inch) piece fresh ginger, peeled and minced

2 Indian green chilies, minced, seeds and all! (see Notes)

1 teaspoon turmeric powder

½ teaspoon garam masala (optional)

1 (15-ounce) can low-sodium chickpeas (see Notes)

½ teaspoon kosher salt

Pinch of freshly ground black pepper

1 teaspoon fresh lemon juice

2 tablespoons coarsely chopped fresh cilantro (stems and all!)

Italian or French baguette, sliced in ½-inch-thick slices on the diagonal

Olive oil

2 to 3 tablespoons pomegranate seeds

Handful of fresh cilantro leaves

¼ wedge fresh lemon

Method follows

MAKE THE YOGURT SAUCE: Using a whisk, mix together yogurt, lemon zest, sugar, salt, cumin, and black pepper in a small bowl until smooth and lump-free. Give it a taste and add more salt if necessary. It should be a balance of sweet and tangy, with a slight smokiness from the cumin. Wrap the bowl with plastic wrap (or an airtight lid) and place in the refrigerator until ready to serve, or up to 7 days.

MAKE THE MASALA CHICKPEAS: Using a mortar and pestle, grind the fennel seeds and coriander seeds together until coarsely ground. Place a medium nonstick pan over medium-high heat. Pour in the neutral oil and, once hot, add the crushed fennel-coriander seed mixture. Sauté for 30 seconds until fragrant. Add the onion, garlic, ginger, and chilies. Sauté for 3 to 4 minutes, until the onion starts sweating and becomes translucent. The mixture should become very fragrant. Add the turmeric and garam masala, if using, and mix together well until all the onion mixture is coated. Cook for another 2 to 3 minutes. If the mixture starts to look a bit clumpy, stir in 1 tablespoon water. Now add the chickpeas and incorporate well into the mixture. Sauté for about 5 minutes, until the chickpeas begin to soften. Add the salt, pepper, and lemon juice. Cook for another 5 minutes. Once the chickpeas are soft, but still have a bit of a bite, reduce the heat to low and, using a potato masher, mash about a quarter of the mixture. The mixture should be textured but still have some whole pieces of chickpea. Taste for salt, as it might need more! At this point, turn off the heat and add the cilantro. Set aside to cool.

LET'S GET TOASTY: Set a large nonstick skillet over medium-high heat. While the skillet heats up, drizzle the sliced baguette with olive oil and toast each side until golden brown but not too dark. Transfer to a platter.

LET'S ASSEMBLE: Dollop ½ to 1 tablespoon of the yogurt mixture on each slice of toasted baguette. Top each with a generous heaping of the Masala Chickpea mixture. Garnish with the pomegranate seeds, cilantro, and a squeeze of lemon juice. These bruschetta travel well—the texture of the chickpeas and yogurt allows the baguette to retain its crunch.

✕ ────────────────────────────

NOTES: Green arbol chili peppers or serrano chili peppers can be substituted for Indian green chilies.

See Notes on reducing waste by repurposing the chickpea liquid from the can, page 39.

Bucatini à la Pumpkin with Pink Peppercorn & Pistachio

⇴ SERVES 2 ⇴

Do you have a favorite pasta shape? Come on, we all do. My sisters and I used to always make fun of my parents, because whenever we went out to eat Italian food, they would always ask for "bowties with pesto primavera," even if it wasn't on the menu. So, you can say farfalle aka bowties were my parents' favorite shape. But, back to me. Without question, my favorite pasta shape is bucatini—simple, hearty, and efficient. Why is it efficient? Well, it has all the fun and silliness of spaghetti, but it's equipped with this hollow tube that is a perfect vessel for sucking up delicious sauce. It's a win-win in my pasta book!

And what better way to pair bucatini than with a deliciously unique sauce made from pumpkin, pink peppercorn, and pistachio? The creaminess of the pumpkin seeps right on into the bucatini, so every bite is super flavorful. And the pink peppercorn adds a delicate and flowery sweetness. Plus you know I never make a recipe without varying textures, so the pistachios add a buttery crunch that balances the whole dish out. This dish tastes fabulous crisped up in a pan the next day so, if you do have leftovers (which I'm assuming you won't), not to worry, because nothing will go to waste!

2 hefty pinches kosher salt

1 tablespoon plus 1 teaspoon olive oil

6 ounces bucatini pasta

1 teaspoon pink peppercorns

3 tablespoons unsalted pistachios, coarsely chopped

2 tablespoons vegan butter

½ teaspoon red pepper flakes

1 small yellow onion, diced

2 cloves garlic, minced

½ (15-ounce) can organic pumpkin puree

¼ cup nondairy cream cheese

Pinch of freshly ground black pepper

⅛ teaspoon freshly grated nutmeg

BOIL THAT PASTA: In a large skillet, pour in water, leaving about ½ inch from the rim. Set over high heat to bring to a boil. Add 1 hefty pinch of salt and the 1 teaspoon oil. Once the water is boiling, add the bucatini, making sure to spread it evenly in the water. Boil for 8 to 10 minutes.

GRIND THE SPICES: In a mortar and pestle, grind together the peppercorns and pistachios until coarsely ground and incorporated. Set aside.

Method continues

LET'S GET SAUCY: While the pasta boils, make the sauce. Set another large pan over medium heat and add the 1 tablespoon oil. Once the oil is shimmering and has ripples, it's hot. Add 1 tablespoon of the vegan butter and, once it melts, add 1 teaspoon of the peppercorn-pistachio mixture and the red pepper flakes. Once fragrant, add the onion and garlic. Sauté, making sure to mix the butter well through the onion and garlic mixture, and cook for 3 to 4 minutes, until the onion becomes translucent. Once the garlic is golden, lower the heat to medium-low, and add the pumpkin puree and cream cheese. Stir to incorporate thoroughly, making sure to break down the cream cheese until the sauce looks cohesive. Add 1 hefty pinch of salt, a pinch of pepper, and the nutmeg. Stir in ¼ cup pasta water. Reduce the heat to low and let the sauce simmer for 2 to 3 minutes, until a slow bubbling appears. Taste and adjust for salt if necessary.

FINAL PRODUCT: After 8 to 10 minutes, once the pasta is al dente (soft yet still has a bite, or the classic Martha Stewart test—when thrown at a steel refrigerator and sticks, it's ready!), add the pasta to the pumpkin sauce and toss to coat. Simmer for 2 minutes to seep in the flavors. Add another ¼ cup pasta water to make for a creamy sauce. Mix in the remaining 1 tablespoon vegan butter; this will make the sauce silky. Garnish with the remaining peppercorn-pistachio mixture and serve. If traveling, add an extra ladle of pasta water to the sauce before packing up in your tiffin. This helps retain a creamy texture even if it's cooled down to room temperature.

✂ ————————————————————

TIP: This pasta tastes great as leftovers converted into a "pizza." Heat a small nonstick skillet over high heat. Add 1 teaspoon olive oil and, once hot, add the leftover pasta. Cook, reducing the heat to medium-high. After about 5 minutes, the bottom should be golden brown. Using a spatula, flip the pasta to cook on the other side for another 5 minutes, until golden brown and crispy. Slide onto a platter and let rest for 2 minutes before cutting into slices. Serve with a dollop of nondairy sour cream. Enjoy!

Cauliflower-Saffron Pasta

⇒ SERVES 2 ⇐

I've traveled to Italy a few times in my life and have visited most regions: the north, the center, and the south. There is one ingredient that periodically showed up in savory dishes regardless of where I was, and that is saffron. I saw it used in seafood dishes (which I obviously did not partake of), and I saw it in a few fresh pasta and risotto dishes. And, for all the obvious reasons—because, let's be honest, who has ever said that they DON'T like saffron—I loved it! The use of saffron in Italian food is truly that combo of Italian meeting Eastern flavors—yes, the origins of saffron are somewhat disputed, but the name is derived from the Sanskrit word *kunkumam*, which indicates the yellow hue that saffron produces.

I was inspired by these dishes that I saw in Italy and, of course, had to create my own. This Cauliflower-Saffron Pasta combines a few Italian and Eastern/Indian elements—tagliatelle, a classic Italian pasta shape, and parsley, a fresh Italian herb, meet saffron, cauliflower, red chili, and cinnamon—common ingredients used throughout various Indian dishes. So, does this dish transport you to the mixed Eurasian culture that once existed?

Pinch of kosher salt

1 tablespoon olive oil, plus more for drizzling

8 ounces tagliatelle pasta

1 small head cauliflower

2 tablespoons unsalted raw pine nuts

2 cloves garlic, minced

½ teaspoon red pepper flakes

1 teaspoon saffron threads

Pinch of good-quality ground cinnamon

Pinch of freshly ground black pepper

1 tablespoon vegan butter, at room temperature

¼ cup chopped fresh flat-leaf parsley

COOK THE PASTA: Fill a large pot three-quarters full of water, sprinkle with a hefty pinch of salt, drizzle with some oil, and bring to a boil over high heat. Once boiling, add the tagliatelle and boil until al dente, 7 to 10 minutes. Drain, but reserve the pasta water and set aside.

MEANWHILE, PREPARE THE CAULIFLOWER: Cut the cauliflower into ½-inch pieces. Alternatively, you can blitz the cauliflower in a food processor, but we want to avoid turning it into a cauliflower "rice."

TOAST THE PINE NUTS: In a small skillet, toast the pine nuts over medium-low heat for 3 to 4 minutes, until lightly golden. Set aside.

TIME TO SAUTÉ: In a large nonstick skillet, add the 1 tablespoon oil and set over medium heat. Once hot, add the garlic and red pepper flakes. Sauté for 30 seconds, then add the cauliflower and toss to coat. Cook for 5 to 8 minutes, until there is some golden color on the cauliflower and it starts to get tender. Separately in a small bowl, mix together 2 tablespoons of the reserved warm pasta water and the saffron threads. Let soak. Once the water has turned a beautiful yellow-orange, pour the saffron water—threads and all—into the sautéed cauliflower, add a pinch of cinnamon, and toss. Cook for 5 to 7 minutes, until the cauliflower becomes fork-tender.

PASTA TIME: Using tongs, add the pasta to the cauliflower mixture along with ¼ cup reserved pasta water and toss well. Let the pasta seep in the flavors of the cauliflower sauce for 3 to 4 minutes. This will not be a thick, creamy sauce. Add a pinch of salt and pepper, the vegan butter, and half of the parsley. Toss everything together until just combined.

GARNISH AND SERVE: Garnish with the remaining parsley and the pine nuts. Serve and stuff your face! If traveling, add an extra ¼ cup pasta water before packing in your tiffin. This allows the pasta to retain its texture without getting too dry once cooled down to room temperature.

Indian Stuffed Mushrooms

⫸ SERVES 2 TO 4 ⫷

I have a confession. I'm in love with the fungi. There, I said it. Mushrooms are the best—they grow in the dark, are literally a fungus, but are PACKED with protein, vitamins, minerals, and antioxidants. Not to mention, they make a great vessel to pick up flavors, and plant-based converts love them because they have a slightly meaty texture. I can't let this recipe introduction go by without also mentioning that mushrooms are the wave of the future—there are over fifty thousand species of mushrooms and counting, and many are able to help break down and consume plastic, consume harmful bacteria that afflict vegetation, and much more. Need I say more on the magnificence that is the fungus?! Fun fact: my dad HATES mushrooms and tells waitstaff at restaurants that he's "allergic" (my sisters and I think he's lying, but I digress. He will likely get mad while reading this!). Perhaps that's why I like mushrooms. Because my dad has such an adverse reaction, I decided, "Heck, let me try these things!" And immediately fell in love. But you're probably wondering what this has to do with stuffed mushrooms. Nothing really, I just wanted to express my love for fungus. This dish combines a lot of delicious elements familiar to Indian cooking but is built off the Italian concept of stuffed artichokes (which I absolutely love and ate a ton of growing up on Staten Island). These are perfect as a light lunch, appetizer, or snack. I say this serves two to four people if you're being nice, but honestly, you may just eat them all yourself!

- 1 (10-ounce) package baby portobello mushrooms
- ½ teaspoon cumin seeds
- ½ teaspoon coriander seeds
- 2 teaspoons olive oil, plus more for drizzling
- 3 scallions, thinly sliced
- 2 cloves garlic, minced
- 1 serrano chili pepper, minced
- 1 teaspoon fresh lemon zest
- ½ cup plain unsalted bread crumbs
- ½ fresh lemon
- Kosher salt and freshly ground black pepper
- 3 heaping tablespoons coarsely chopped fresh cilantro (stems and all!)

PREHEAT THE OVEN to 350°F.

CLEAN THE MUSHROOMS: Using a damp kitchen or paper towel, clean the mushrooms' tops, stems, sides, all around. Remove the stems from the caps and set aside.

SPICE IT UP: In a mortar and pestle, coarsely grind together the cumin seeds and coriander seeds.

SAUTÉ: In a medium nonstick skillet, heat the 2 teaspoons oil over medium heat. Once hot, add the scallions, garlic, serrano, mushroom stems, and coriander-cumin mixture. Sauté for 3 to 4 minutes until fragrant, then add the lemon zest and bread crumbs. Toss to incorporate everything and cook for another 2 to 3 minutes, until the bread crumbs turn golden brown and crispy. Lastly, squeeze the lemon over the bread crumb mixture and add 1 tablespoon water until the mixture is just moistened (if not, add another tablespoon of water). Season with a pinch of salt and pepper and toss. Remove from the heat and give it a quick taste—add more salt if necessary. Add 1 tablespoon of the cilantro and toss.

STUFF AND BAKE: Line a baking sheet with parchment paper. Place the mushrooms onto the pan, cavity side up, drizzle with oil, and sprinkle with salt and pepper. Using a spoon, generously stuff each mushroom cavity with the bread crumb mixture until it's piled high. Drizzle a little more oil over the bread crumb portion of the stuffed mushrooms and bake for 10 to 15 minutes, until the mushrooms are fork-tender and the filling is browned. Remove from the oven and let cool for 2 minutes.

GARNISH AND SERVE: Sprinkle with the remaining 2 tablespoons cilantro and serve. These taste perfect at room temperature, so it's a great treat to pack for on-the-go!

Lemon Risotto with Tempered Spices

⇒⊱ SERVES 2 ⇷⇐

Okay, I have to admit—this is probably the weirdest dish in this chapter. But when was weird ever a bad thing? In my life, being weird has generally paid off, so here goes! This dish combines a few elements: a distinct experience I had eating lemon risotto on a seaside cliff on the Amalfi Coast, a traditional South Indian lemon peanut rice, and my family's obsession with risotto. In 2017, while visiting one of my closest friends, Vesselina, who was living in Italy at the time, I tasted some of the best lemon risotto of my life—delicate, creamy, not too overpowering of lemon. It was perfect, and to add to the experience, we were sitting on a cliffside facing the Tyrrhenian Sea. Next, South Indian lemon peanut rice is a rice I enjoy—and if you know me by now, I'm one of those "weird" Indians who *really* doesn't fancy rice, so that means this is *good*. Sautéed with black mustard seeds, peanuts, lots of turmeric, and lemon, this rice is vibrant, fragrant, and delicious. And of course, Maa makes it the best. And lastly, yes, my family is obsessed with risotto. Why? Because it's creamy, flavorful, and it's RICE! My family loves rice! And we had the pleasure of having a family friend, Giampiero, a vivacious Italian gentleman, teach us traditional Italian cooking techniques, one of which was risotto. And ever since, we've been hooked. This Lemon Risotto with Tempered Spices is a true culmination of all three of those life experiences—Italian adventure, classic Indian home cooking, and traditional Italian cooking technique. What do you think?

3 cups low-sodium vegetable broth, plus more if necessary

1 tablespoon vegan butter, plus 1 teaspoon for garnish

1 tablespoon olive oil

1 medium yellow onion, diced

2 cloves garlic, minced

¼ teaspoon red pepper flakes

Kosher salt

⅔ cup arborio rice

¼ cup dry white wine

1 teaspoon fresh lemon zest, plus a pinch for garnish

½ fresh lemon

Freshly ground black pepper

TEMPERED SPICES

1 tablespoon olive oil

2 dried red chilies

½ teaspoon black mustard seeds

1 tablespoon unsalted raw slivered almonds

WARM THE BROTH: In a medium saucepan, place the vegetable broth over low heat. Keep warm over the stove—do not let it boil.

RISOTTO TIME: Place a large pot over medium-low heat and add the 1 tablespoon vegan butter and the oil. Once melted, add the onion and garlic. Sauté for about 1 minute, and then add the red pepper flakes and a pinch of salt. Sauté for another 2 to 3 minutes, until the onion begins to sweat and becomes translucent. Once that happens, add the arborio rice, toss to coat with the onion mixture, and toast for about 2 minutes. Mix in the white wine—if the liquid is getting absorbed too quickly, lower the heat. The liquid should slowly evaporate and incorporate into the rice, allowing the rice to cook and plump up (this takes time).

BROTH TIME: Once the wine has cooked into the rice, add the lemon zest and the juice from the lemon (being careful to not get the seeds in). Stir to incorporate. Add 1 ladle of warm broth into the rice and stir. Once the broth is slightly absorbed, add another ladle and stir. Repeat this for about 30 minutes, until the rice is cooked through and the risotto is creamy. The key is not to let the rice become dry, but also not to overwhelm it with too much broth. So you must consistently stir for even cooking. If you find that the broth has been used up but the rice still needs to cook, add more warm broth and mix until the rice is creamy, soft, and cooked. Add a pinch of salt and a few grinds of pepper. Mix, taste, and add more salt if necessary. Remove from the heat, top with the 1 teaspoon butter, and let it melt. Add a pinch of lemon zest. Divide between two shallow dinner bowls.

TEMPER THE SPICES: In a small skillet, heat the 1 tablespoon oil over medium-high heat. Once the oil has ripples, it's hot! Add the red chilies (without breaking up) and mustard seeds and let sizzle and pop for about 30 seconds. Add the almonds and toss until they color slightly. Remove from the heat. Using a spoon, divide the tempered spices over the top of the risotto.

TIPS FOR MAKING YOUR RISOTTO PORTABLE: Add an extra ladle of broth to your risotto right as it is finishing to cook—it should be on the "runny" side so when the risotto cools to room temperature, it can retain the texture that it would have if served immediately. Top it with the tempered spices and pack it in your tiffin. If your tiffin is not insulated, I recommend placing it in an insulated bag to retain as much heat as possible. Then you can be on your way!

FOUR

The
AMERICAN COMFORT
TIFFIN

Masala Grilled Cheese

78

Creamy Grits with
Roasted Tomato Jam

80

Corn Bread Gulab Jamun

82

Tadka Mac 'n' Cheese with
Cajun Bread Crumbs

84

Chili-Maple Skillet Corn Bread

86

I am 100 percent one of those New Yorkers who has not visited the heartland of America or much of the South. To be honest, these areas are on my list to visit, but when it comes down to buying tickets, it costs the same to fly to New Orleans as it does to Barcelona! This is a true story—my friends and I were looking up domestic travel options, and the flight from NYC to New Orleans was the same price as NYC to Barcelona, SPAIN. It's almost like they (and, by they, I mean airlines, corporations, government—you know, "they") don't want Americans to travel domestically, or New Yorkers, at least. But aside from the economic factor, traveling to the heartland of the country or even the South is a bit intimidating. If you all haven't guessed by now, I'm Indian, which means I look different and I'm not always sure that I would be welcomed with open arms in some of these states. But that doesn't stop me from *wanting* to go and, especially, from wanting to experience the food. This is a cookbook after all, so back to the food!

My American Comfort chapter is a culmination of dishes that I experienced either in my home state, as "American food" growing up, or while traveling through America. It also represents what I *think* of as traditional American food. But isn't modern-day America built on immigrants anyway? So, the interpretation of this chapter can run wild and free (see what I did there?)!

Masala Grilled Cheese

⇒⟫ SERVES 2 ⟪⇐

I think we can all agree that grilled cheese is a classic American dish, and no one can dispute that it is comforting as h*ll! If my memory serves me well, I'm pretty sure I once read (when doing research on grilled cheese, because isn't that what we all do on the weekends?) that grilled cheese originated during the World War II era, specifically during the Great Depression, for the armed forces. So, yes! One of the most nostalgic and comforting foods to Americans comes from a financial and social crisis in modern-day history!

But enough about that, let's talk Masala Grilled Cheese. By now you should know that I love putting my own twist on tradition. I always love taking my grilled cheese up a notch—whether by spreading a spicy chutney that my mom made in between the bread and cheese or adding some fresh cilantro, there is always some Indian element that I add. So, this Masala Grilled Cheese combines all the comfort that you're familiar with in a grilled cheese, but with a golden mayo-based crust (don't knock it till you try it!), caramelized onions (because that just screams comfort to me), and spicy red chili (because there is no way I am eating a bland grilled cheese). I hope this Masala Grilled Cheese becomes a comforting staple in your household!

CARAMELIZED KASHMIRI RED CHILI ONIONS

- ¼ teaspoon fennel seeds
- 1 teaspoon olive oil
- 1 teaspoon vegan butter
- 1 small yellow onion, thinly sliced
- Pinch of kosher salt
- ¼ teaspoon Kashmiri red chili powder
- Pinch of freshly ground nutmeg

CREAMY KASHMIRI RED CHILI DIP

- ¼ cup plain nondairy cream cheese
- 2 tablespoons unsweetened plain nondairy yogurt
- Pinch of Kashmiri red chili powder
- Kosher salt and freshly ground black pepper
- 1 teaspoon neutral oil
- 1 whole Kashmiri chili
- ⅛ teaspoon cumin seeds
- Pinch of raw cane sugar (optional)

MASALA GRILLED CHEESE

- 2 tablespoons vegan mayonnaise
- 1 tablespoon coarsely chopped fresh cilantro (stems and all!)
- ⅛ teaspoon cumin seeds
- 4 slices crusty sourdough or ciabatta bread
- 4 slices vegan smoked Gouda
- 4 slices vegan yellow cheddar

FOR GARNISH

- 1 cup baby arugula
- Olive oil, for drizzling
- ¼ wedge fresh lemon

CARAMELIZE THE ONION: Coarsely grind the fennel seeds in a mortar and pestle. Set aside. Place a medium nonstick skillet over medium-low heat. Add the olive oil and vegan butter. Once it starts to melt, add the onion and a small pinch of salt. Sauté until translucent, about 2 minutes, then reduce the heat to low. Sprinkle in the red chili powder, ground fennel seeds, and nutmeg. Cook for about 10 minutes, until the onion becomes soft, caramelized, and golden brown. Remove from the skillet and set aside. Do not rinse the skillet.

MAKE THE DIPPING SAUCE: Place the cream cheese, yogurt, red chili powder, and a small pinch of salt and pepper in a blender. Blend until smooth and creamy. Transfer to a small dipping bowl. Set the smallest pan you have over medium-high heat and pour in the neutral oil. Once the oil has ripples and is shimmering—it's hot!—carefully add the Kashmiri chili and the cumin seeds. Allow to pop and become fragrant, for about 30 seconds. Remove and immediately add it to the dipping sauce and stir. Taste and if it needs salt, add it! If it's too tart, add a small pinch of sugar and stir. Set aside until ready to serve.

GRILL THE CHEESE: Rinse out the blender that was used for the dipping sauce. Place the vegan mayonnaise, cilantro, and cumin seeds in the blender. Blend until very smooth, with no visible lumps or leaves. Place the 4 slices of bread flat onto a cutting board and spread the mayonnaise mixture evenly across one side of each slice. Next, place the same skillet used for the onion on the stove over medium heat. There should be residual oil in the skillet. Once the skillet is hot, place 2 slices of the bread into the skillet, mayonnaise side down. Layer 2 slices each of smoked Gouda and cheddar onto each side, plus about 1 heaping tablespoon of caramelized onion. Cover with the other slice of bread, mayonnaise side up. Cover the skillet with a lid to allow the steam to aid in melting the vegan cheese. After about 2 minutes, the bottom slice should be golden brown, so carefully flip to the other side and cook for another 2 to 3 minutes, uncovered, until golden brown. Remove from the heat.

GARNISH AND SERVE: In a medium bowl, toss the arugula with a drizzle of olive oil and a squeeze of lemon juice. Slice the grilled cheeses in half and place on a serving dish. Top generously with the arugula mixture and serve with the Creamy Kashmiri Red Chili Dip. If traveling, place the arugula inside a sandwich before covering with the second slice of bread. It will add a fresh peppery bite once bitten into on the road!

Creamy Grits with Roasted Tomato Jam

⇒ SERVES 2 ⇐

I'm not sure about you, but I grew up on instant grits—I am talking the Quaker Oats Instant Grits packets. I have no idea what it is about grits, but I absolutely love the creaminess, the warmth, and the fact that they are a vessel for deliciously sweet toppings. This was definitely a preferred breakfast of mine on cold mornings before heading to school. I think my grits-loving gene comes from Maa, as she loves them, too. And I know grits are a staple in the South; I have traveled and eaten in Georgia enough to know that grits popped up in nearly every restaurant I visited, and I sure as hell was not complaining! I've tasted grits with butter and sugar, grits with cheddar and jalapeño, grits with maple—you name it, I've probably eaten it! Sans meat, of course.

My Creamy Grits with Roasted Tomato Jam packs in all the comfort of traditional grits but brings along a little punch to wake up your senses! Think of it as a Southern gal who escaped to the big city. I also love that this can be easily packed and eaten at room temperature—perfectly delicious!

TANGY TOMATO JAM
2 teaspoons olive oil

1 cup cherry or grape tomatoes, rinsed thoroughly

1 clove garlic, minced

1 jalapeño, diced (seeds and all!)

¼ teaspoon kosher salt, plus more for seasoning

2 teaspoons light agave

1 tablespoon tamarind chutney (see Note)

1 sprig fresh thyme

Pinch of freshly ground nutmeg

⅛ teaspoon freshly ground black pepper

1 scallion, thinly sliced on the bias, white and green parts separated

CREAMY GRITS
¾ cup stone-ground corn grits

¾ cup unsweetened plain nondairy creamer

¼ cup nondairy sour cream, at room temperature

¼ teaspoon cumin powder

¼ teaspoon kosher salt, plus more for seasoning

Pinch of freshly ground black pepper

1 tablespoon vegan butter

MAKE THE JAM: Place the oil in a small pot set over medium heat. Once the oil is shimmering and has ripples, it's hot! Add the tomatoes. Give them a stir to make sure all the tomatoes are coated with the oil and sizzling. After 1 minute, add the garlic, jalapeños, and salt and sauté for another 2 to 3 minutes, until the tomatoes start blistering and breaking open. Lower the heat to medium-low and, using the back of a fork, start mashing the tomatoes until the juices come out. Add the agave, chutney, thyme, nutmeg, and black pepper. If the mixture is very thick and slightly sticking to the pot, add up to 2 tablespoons water. Stir, reduce the heat to low, and cover. Simmer for 5 minutes, until the mixture thickens to a jammy consistency and the tomatoes have completely softened. Stir and taste. Add a pinch of salt, if necessary, and discard the sprig of thyme. Remove from the heat, stir in the white parts of the scallion, and set aside to cool.

MAKE THE GRITS: In a large pot, bring the grits and 1 cup water to a boil over medium-high heat, stirring constantly with a wooden spoon. Once the mixture is slightly bubbling and the grits are swelling up, reduce the heat to low and cover. Cook for 5 to 8 minutes, until the grits are "al dente." Add the creamer, sour cream, cumin, salt, and pepper and stir until fully incorporated. Remove from the heat and taste, and add more salt if necessary. If you're traveling, add an additional ¼ cup water to the grits at this stage. Lastly, top with the vegan butter and give it a slight stir.

SERVE IT UP: Divide the grits between two bowls or into a tiffin section. Top with the Tangy Tomato Jam and garnish with the green parts of the scallion. This dish travels well and is perfectly delicious at room temperature!

NOTE: See the Glossary (page 194) on buying the best store-bought chutneys and some of my favorite brands.

Corn Bread Gulab Jamun

⇛ SERVES 2 (15 TO 18 GULAB JAMUNS) ⇚

If I could eat one type of meal for the rest of my life, it would probably be a dessert. If I had to narrow it down further to a dessert that only Maa makes the best, it would 100 percent be her gulab jamun. A staple of Indian cuisine, these slightly dense, yet fluffy fritters are made of dried milk, flour, and cardamom fried to a crisp and soaked in a luscious saffron syrup. If anyone tells you they *don't* like gulab jamun, it just means they haven't tried it, because I can assure you, it's life-changing. There is nothing not to like about it except that it can be a bit on the laborious side to make and just a tad bit on the indulgent side. I wanted to create something that was nostalgic but fit into my lifestyle. Thus, these delicious Corn Bread Gulab Jamuns were born. The addition of cornmeal is *so* American, and the stovetop skillet preparation removes the need for deep-frying, although you do need an aebleskiver pan. These are simple to make and provide the same feelings as if you were eating the traditional decadent gulab jamun. Even better—you can prepare all the components ahead of time and pack it with you wherever you go!

CORN BREAD GULAB JAMUNS
- ¼ cup vegetable oil or coconut oil, plus more for coating the pan
- ¾ cup cornmeal
- ½ cup all-purpose flour
- 1 teaspoon baking powder
- ¼ teaspoon kosher salt
- 1 tablespoon raw cane sugar
- ¼ teaspoon freshly ground cardamom, plus more for garnish
- 1 cup unsweetened nondairy milk
- Dried rose petals, for garnish (optional)

SAFFRON SYRUP
- ½ cup raw cane sugar
- Pinch of saffron threads

MAKE THE SAFFRON SYRUP: Place the sugar and saffron with ½ cup water in a small heavy-bottom pot over medium-high heat. Bring to a boil, stirring to dissolve the sugar. Reduce the heat to low and simmer until thickened to a syrupy consistency. You can check this by stirring with a steel spoon and lifting the spoon to watch the droplets. If the drops stretch like maple syrup, it's ready! Remove from the heat to cool completely.

BATTER UP THE GULAB JAMUN: In a large bowl, add all of the ingredients and whisk together until well combined with no visible lumps or streaks. Do not overmix! The consistency should be similar to a pancake batter.

COOK 'EM UP: Place an aebleskiver pan over medium heat. The pan will take a minute to heat up—you can test to see if it is hot by adding a little droplet of batter and checking if it sizzles up and cooks. Once hot, add ¼ teaspoon oil into each circle of the pan. Pour the batter into each round about three-quarters of the way up. Cook for 3 to 5 minutes on one side, then turn using a spoon. It should be golden brown. If not, turn back around and let the gulab jamuns cook a bit more. If there is a lot of smoke coming off the pan, lower the heat to medium-low. Cook on the other side for another 2 to 3 minutes, until golden brown. Remove, cool, and repeat until all the batter is used.

SOAK 'EM: Spread most of the saffron syrup on the bottom of a serving dish. Pile the gulab jamuns on top. Drizzle with another tablespoon of the syrup on top. Garnish with the rose petals, if using, and cardamom. If packing your jamuns up for an adventure, place a spoonful of saffron syrup on the bottom of your tiffin, stack in the gulab jamuns, and top with more saffron syrup. The syrup will soak into the jamuns so by the time you eat them, they will be very flavorful and luscious.

Tadka Mac 'n' Cheese with Cajun Bread Crumbs

⇒ SERVES 2 ⇐

Have you ever met anyone in your life who does not like macaroni and cheese? Like they can look at you and say, straight to your face, "I do not like macaroni and cheese." No? Yup, same. I have never met anyone who does not like macaroni and cheese, and if they say that they don't, they definitely cannot be trusted and should be reported to the authorities.

This is another American classic that just oozes comfort—the smell, the sound, the taste—everything. My mom made my sisters and me macaroni and cheese and paired it with homemade chakli—popular fried spicy Indian snacks made out of chickpea flour, red chili, and spices. It tasted so good. The spice of the chakli cut through the creaminess of the cheese, so it was the perfect balance. My Tadka Mac 'n' Cheese with Cajun Bread Crumbs is an ode to the delicious mac 'n' cheese with chakli that we grew up eating. And in case you all don't have chakli at home, this is the closest thing! I love this dish because it not only provides the creamy comfort of a traditional macaroni, but it has a crispy texture from the bread crumbs, and the tempered spices add just the oomph that a traditional macaroni and cheese is yearning for! Have I convinced you to make this yet?

MAC 'N' CHEESE
8 ounces elbow macaroni

Kosher salt

1 tablespoon neutral oil

¼ teaspoon cumin seeds, or ½ teaspoon cumin powder

3 curry leaves (optional)

2 Indian green chilies, minced (see Note)

1 medium yellow onion, diced

3 cloves garlic, minced

1 hefty teaspoon turmeric powder

2 tablespoons vegan butter, plus more for the pan

1 tablespoon all-purpose flour

1 cup unsweetened full-fat plain oat milk

¼ cup plain nondairy cream cheese

1 cup shredded vegan cheddar

¼ cup shredded vegan mozzarella

¼ cup shredded vegan pepper jack

Pinch of freshly ground black pepper

2 tablespoons coarsely chopped fresh cilantro (stems and all!)

CAJUN BREAD CRUMB TOPPING
½ cup plain unsalted panko bread crumbs

¼ teaspoon Kashmiri red chili powder

½ teaspoon paprika

¼ teaspoon garlic powder

¼ teaspoon dried oregano

Pinch of dried thyme

Hefty pinch of kosher salt

Pinch of freshly ground black pepper

2 teaspoons olive oil

COOK THE PASTA: Bring a medium pot of water to a rolling boil and add a hefty pinch of salt. Add the elbow macaroni and cook according to package directions until al dente. Drain, reserving 1 cup pasta water. Set aside.

LET'S GET SPICY: In a large heavy-bottom pan, pour in the neutral oil and set over medium-high heat. Once the oil is hot, add the cumin seeds and allow them to sizzle and pop for 30 seconds. Then add the curry leaves, if using, and stand back, as they aggressively pop. Once the popping subsides, lower the heat to medium and add the green chilies, onion, and garlic. Sauté for about 2 minutes, until the onion looks translucent and starts to sweat. Add the turmeric and toss to coat. Lower the heat to medium-low.

LET'S GET CHEESY: Add the 2 tablespoons vegan butter and the flour and whisk together with the onion mixture to create a roux. Once the roux has a nutty aroma and is slightly golden and clumpy, pour in the oat milk and continue to whisk. After 1 to 2 minutes, after the mixture has thickened to a béchamel consistency—a good test is dipping in a steel spoon and running your finger down the back; if the sauce doesn't bleed into the middle of your spoon, it's ready—add the nondairy cream cheese and whisk until completely blended. Next, add the shredded vegan cheeses and whisk. Notice we have no added salt yet! Once you have a thick cheese sauce, taste for salt. Add if necessary—the vegan cheeses tend to be on the saltier side, so add salt cautiously. Add a pinch of pepper. Then switch to a spatula, add the elbow macaroni, and toss to coat completely. If the pasta looks too thick and is sticking together, add some of the reserved pasta water. Butter a medium baking dish or casserole dish and pour in the macaroni and cheese.

MAKE THE BREAD CRUMB TOPPING: Preheat the oven to 350°F. In a small bowl, toss together the bread crumbs with all of the seasonings and the olive oil until well coated and incorporated. Top the macaroni and cheese with the bread crumbs. Bake, uncovered, for 10 minutes. Broil for another 2 minutes until the bread crumbs are golden brown and the macaroni and cheese is slightly bubbling.

GARNISH AND SERVE: Remove from the oven and place on a rack to cool for 2 minutes. Top with the cilantro and place on individual serving dishes or directly into your tiffin. This remains perfectly creamy even when cooled down to room temperature!

✕ ────────────────────────

NOTE: Green arbol chili peppers or serrano chili peppers can be substituted for Indian green chilies.

Chili-Maple Skillet Corn Bread

⇛ SERVES 2 ⇚

I think this is another one of those genes from Maa that was transferred to me—the corn gene. I like to make corny jokes and I love corn-filled dishes. And I absolutely love corn bread. What is it about corn bread? Perhaps it's the crumb or the fact that it's served in a cast-iron skillet or that I ate one too many corn muffins growing up (oh yeah, a huge corn muffin from a local NYC deli, cut in half, toasted, with some margarine—if you're not drooling from that description, just close this book). Either way, I couldn't write this book without including one of the all-time favorite American classics—skillet corn bread. I'm pretty sure corn (or maize) was discovered, planted, and harvested by American Indians and the first appearance of corn bread was within indigenous culture. So, corn bread is THE OG American dish.

My Chili-Maple Skillet Corn Bread is not only the perfect size, but it combines spicy earthiness with the sweetness of maple syrup and the freshness of corn. It's perfect!

CORN BREAD

1 tablespoon vegan butter, at room temperature

¾ cup cornmeal

½ cup all-purpose flour

1 teaspoon baking powder

½ teaspoon kosher salt

1 teaspoon raw cane sugar

¾ cup unsweetened nondairy milk

¼ cup neutral oil

1 teaspoon garam masala (page 200)

1 tablespoon coarsely chopped fresh cilantro (stems and all!), plus a few leaves for garnish

1 Indian green chili, minced (see Note)

MAPLE-CHILI GARLIC BUTTER

4 tablespoons vegan butter, at room temperature

1 clove garlic, coarsely chopped

1 Indian green chili, chopped

1 tablespoon coarsely chopped fresh cilantro (stems and all!)

⅛ teaspoon amchur (mango) powder (optional)

Pinch of kosher salt

Pinch of freshly ground black pepper

PREP YOUR SKILLET: Preheat the oven to 350°F. Grease a small cast-iron skillet or baking dish with vegan butter. Set aside.

BATTER UP: In a medium mixing bowl, using a wooden spoon or whisk, mix together all of the corn bread ingredients until just combined—do not overmix.

BAKE: Pour the batter into the prepared pan and bake for 20 to 25 minutes, until cooked through and a toothpick inserted in the center comes out clean. You may see a crack on the top, which is perfectly fine!

MEANWHILE, MAKE THE MAPLE-CHILI GARLIC BUTTER: Using a food processor, blend all of the ingredients together until very smooth with no visible bumps of garlic. Transfer to a small deep bowl and smooth out the top. Place in the fridge to set until ready to serve.

GARNISH AND SERVE: Once the corn bread has cooled for 2 minutes, scoop on some butter using a mini ice-cream scooper and garnish with a few leaves of cilantro. If eating immediately, then serve warm! If packing it up for an adventure, once the corn bread has cooled, cut and place into your tiffin. Separately pack your chilled butter in a small container. By the time you get to your destination, the butter will have become room temperature, so you directly "dunk" your corn bread into the butter and indulge!

✕ ────────────────────────────

NOTE: Green arbol chili peppers or serrano chili peppers can be substituted for the Indian green chilies.

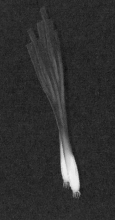

FIVE

The INDO-CHINESE

TIFFIN

L et me guess—you read the title of this chapter and thought, "Yeah, Priyanka definitely made this up. There is no such thing as Indo-Chinese food." I am not completely innocent of making things up, but I promise you, this cuisine is 100 percent real and 100 percent delicious! If you are fortunate enough to visit India at some point in your life, you'll find Indo-Chinese food in a lot of places—Mumbai, Delhi, Belgaum, Calcutta. It's a delicious balance of ingredients familiar to Chinese food, like eggplant, noodles, and tofu, combined with Indian spices and techniques. I'm not going to lie: I cannot tell you the origins of this delicious cuisine—it could have been a random cook in India, who began cooking their idea of Chinese food and then it took off (I 100 percent made this up and this is not true). It's more likely associated with ancient trade routes that traversed from India to China. Clearly, silk wasn't the only good thing being traded!

Indo-Chinese food is super popular in India, and I'm confident that most Indian immigrants and first-generation Indian Americans love Indo-Chinese food in the States, too. So, this chapter is dedicated to the delicious Indo-Chinese food I've eaten throughout India and in Manhattan and Edison, New Jersey—all the epicenters of delicious Indian food!

Tofu 65

⇶ SERVES 2 ⇶

If I tell you the inspiration for this dish, you may be freaked out. Furthermore, if I tell you who told me the origin for this dish and why that is significant, that may freak you out even more! Before I confuse you even further, let's get into it. There is a popular South Indian dish called Chicken 65—it's a white meat piece of chicken that has been marinated in red chili powder, turmeric, and spices and then flash-fried with black mustard seeds, curry leaves, ginger, and garlic. Now, I know what this dish tastes like, because I used to eat chicken (in a former life; I know, so not progressive). But I have to admit, the flavors of this dish are *incredible*. Spicy, zesty, punchy—no wonder it's so popular across India. Now you might be wondering: what does the 65 stand for? Is it 65 spices? I was wondering the same thing, so a long, long time ago I posed this question to my dad . . . now here's where it gets interesting, because my dad has been a strict vegetarian his whole life. So, why would I ask my strict vegetarian dad the origins of a nonvegetarian dish? Because my dad weirdly knows everything. I'm not even joking. He knows everything. So, when I asked him, "Hey, Daddy, what does the 65 stand for in Chicken 65? Is it related to the ingredients or spices?" his response was, "No, it's related to the age of the chicken when they slaughter it, which is why it's so tender in the dish." Yup. Now you can all freak out (and fall over), because if that is the truth, then I am mortified.

There is also the high chance that he was pulling my leg, because he has a tendency to do that and I am the most gullible person on the planet. But whether or not it is true, the true fact of this dish is that the flavors are excellent and have a slight East Asian flair, and that is what I tried to emulate in my Tofu 65. A hint of Indian, a hint of Asian flavors with red chilies, ginger, garlic, fresh cilantro, and a bit of soy sauce—it's the best of both worlds. And most importantly, it's 100 percent cruelty-free and the tofu is certainly not 65 days old.

- 1 **package extra-firm tofu**
- 1 **tablespoon cornstarch**
- 1 **tablespoon plus 3 teaspoons neutral oil**
- ½ **teaspoon black mustard seeds**
- 2 **dried Sichuan red chilies (or dried cayenne peppers)**
- 1 **small red onion, cut into 1-inch cubes**
- 1 **(1-inch) piece fresh ginger, peeled and minced**

- 2 **cloves garlic, minced**
- ½ **teaspoon Kashmiri red chili powder (or any spicy red chili powder)**
- ¼ **teaspoon turmeric powder**
- 1 **tablespoon low-sodium soy sauce**
- ¼ **teaspoon raw cane sugar**
- **Kosher salt (optional)**
- ¼ **cup chopped fresh cilantro (stems and all!)**

PREPARE THE TOFU: It is critical to squeeze all of the moisture from the tofu—this will allow the marinade and flavors to really absorb *into* the tofu. Drain the liquid from the package, wrap the tofu between two thick kitchen towels, and place a heavy cast-iron skillet (or any heavy item) on top of the towel-wrapped tofu. Let rest over a rack on a plate or in the sink to drain out excess moisture. After 10 minutes, remove and pat down with a dry paper towel. Cut into 1-inch cubes and set aside on the cutting board.

MAKE THE MARINADE: In a large bowl, mix together the cornstarch and the 1 tablespoon oil to create a slurry. Add the tofu and toss to coat.

LET'S GET CRISPY: In a large nonstick skillet, add 1 teaspoon oil and place over medium-high heat. Once the oil is hot, add the tofu pieces carefully, as they might splatter from the cornstarch. Cook on each side for about 2 minutes, until golden brown and crispy. Remove and place on a paper towel–lined plate to drain any excess oil.

LET'S GET SAUCY: Using the same large nonstick skillet (there will likely be some tofu and cornstarch bits, and we want that!), add the remaining 2 teaspoons oil to coat the skillet and place over medium-high heat. Once the oil is hot, add the mustard seeds and red chilies. Cook for about 30 seconds, until the popping of the mustard seeds subsides. Then add the onion, ginger, and garlic and sauté for about 5 minutes, until the onion becomes soft, starts sweating, and becomes slightly translucent. Add the red chili powder and turmeric and toss. Once the spices are sticking to the onion, add the soy sauce and 2 to 3 tablespoons water and toss to incorporate. After 1 minute, the sauce should be slightly bubbling. At this point, add the sugar and crispy tofu and toss to coat thoroughly. Give the sauce a quick taste and add salt, if necessary. Cook for another 2 minutes, remove from the heat, and toss in the cilantro.

EAT WITH PLAIN RICE, NOODLES, or even on its own. The longer the tofu sits, the more flavorful it becomes. So, get ready for a jam-packed flavor world when you eat this on the go! My tip is to add some cooked rice to the bottom of your tiffin and then top it with your Tofu 65. That way the rice can act as a flavorful vessel and scoop up all those delicious masalas—yum!

Indo-Chinese Pulao (Fried Rice)

⁂ SERVES 2 ⁂

You've heard of fried rice, right? But did you know different Indian cuisines have fried rice, too, but we don't call it fried rice? It's usually referred to as masala rice or, in Kannada, we call it *wahgarni anna*, which is leftover basmati rice that is flash-fried with whole spices, ground spices, and sometimes onions and fresh cilantro. So, my Indo-Chinese Pulao is a culmination of (American) Chinese fried rice and Indian masala rice—the best of both worlds, eh? Plus, this is a superb way to use up all that rice that you ordered with your takeout (don't lie, I know you're a culprit of over-ordering like the rest of us!). The fun thing about this dish is that you can add whatever veggies you like! You really can't go wrong. As long as you get the balance right between sweet, savory, spicy, crunchy, and salty—you're golden!

- 2 teaspoons neutral oil
- 1 teaspoon toasted sesame oil
- 3 Indian green chilies, slit in half lengthwise
- 2 cloves garlic, sliced
- 1 (½-inch) piece fresh ginger, peeled and sliced
- 1 small yellow onion, diced
- 1 small carrot, diced
- 2 tablespoons unsalted raw cashews, coarsely chopped
- 2 tablespoons green peas

- 1 scallion, thinly sliced on the bias, white and green parts separated
- ¾ cup leftover white rice (see Notes)
- 1 teaspoon low-sodium soy sauce
- ½ teaspoon rice wine vinegar
- 1 teaspoon raw cane sugar
- Pinch of white pepper
- Kosher salt
- 2 tablespoons coarsely chopped fresh cilantro (stems and all!)

MAKE THE VEGGIES: Place a large nonstick skillet over medium-high heat. Pour in the neutral and sesame oils. Once the oil is shimmering with ripples, lower the heat to medium and add the green chilies, garlic, and ginger. Sauté for 30 seconds until fragrant. Add the onion, carrot, and cashews and sauté for 4 to 5 minutes, until the onion becomes translucent. Stir in the peas and the white parts of the scallion.

RICE IT UP: Once the vegetables are fork-tender, add the rice, soy sauce, rice wine vinegar, sugar, and white pepper. Give it a vigorous toss, making sure everything is incorporated and nothing is sticking to the pan. After 1 minute, give it a taste. Add salt if necessary.

GARNISH AND SERVE: Remove from the heat and place into your tiffin or a shallow serving bowl. Garnish with the remaining green part of the scallions and the cilantro. Fun fact: I packed this rice dish for my dad at 8:00 one morning and he said it tasted incredible 5 hours later when he ate it from his tiffin. Needless to say, it packs well!

✗ ———————————————————————

NOTES: This recipe is best when using day-old rice, like leftover rice from takeout/delivery. If you need to make fresh rice, wash ⅓ cup basmati rice in water at least 5 times or until the water runs clear. Soak for 30 minutes. Then pour ⅔ cup water into a small pot, and add the rice and a pinch of salt. Bring to a boil, then lower the heat to a simmer. Cover and cook until fluffy, about 10 minutes. Let cool completely before using for this recipe.

Green arbol chili peppers or serrano chili peppers can be substituted for Indian green chilies.

Chili-Garlic Cashews

➤➤ SERVES 2 ➤➤

I have a confession: I am a cashew-holic. It's true. I am the type to pick out the cashews from an Indian cashew pulao or a Thai sautéed cashew dish, or I'll even stand close to a Nuts 4 Nuts cart in Manhattan just to get a delicious sniff of those caramelized cashews. There's something about cashews—the texture is buttery, but not too buttery; the taste is versatile and can be sweet, spicy, or neutral; and I see cashews pop up in so many global cuisines—it's such a worldly nut!

These Chili-Garlic Cashews bring together two of my favorite things: cashews and Indo-Chinese flavors. It's very common to have masala cashews on hand in Indian households—whole cashews lightly toasted with spices that can be eaten as a snack or with chai. And I love them! My Chili-Garlic Cashews combine the fun of eating masala cashews, but with yummy Indo-Chinese flavors, such as garlic, Sichuan peppercorns, and sugar. So, if you're looking to have a delicious snack on hand, this recipe is for you!

1 dried red chili

¼ teaspoon dried Sichuan peppercorns

¼ teaspoon kosher salt

Pinch of freshly ground black pepper

1 tablespoon light brown sugar

1 teaspoon coconut oil or neutral oil

1 clove garlic, thinly sliced

1 cup unsalted raw cashew nuts

1 tablespoon coarsely chopped fresh cilantro (stems and all!)

MAKE THE SPICE BLEND: In a mortar and pestle, coarsely grind together the red chili, peppercorns, salt, and pepper. Add the brown sugar and mix until fully incorporated with no lumps.

TOAST THE GARLIC: In a small nonstick skillet, heat the oil over medium-low heat. Once the oil is hot with ripples, add the garlic and cook for 30 to 60 seconds, until golden brown. Using tongs, quickly transfer to a paper towel–lined plate to cool completely.

CASHEW TIME: In the same nonstick skillet, add the cashews and toast over medium heat. Keep your eye on it the entire time, as nuts can burn quickly! Reduce the heat to medium-low and keep tossing the cashews so they evenly toast in the skillet. After 1 to 2 minutes, they should begin turning golden. Add the spice mixture and toss to coat completely. Toast for another 2 minutes until fragrant, the cashews are more golden, and the spices have become a deep red/brown. Taste one cashew—be careful, as they'll be hot—for salt. Add more if necessary. Remove from the heat and cool completely for the most flavorful and crispy cashews.

GARNISH AND SERVE: Once the cashews are completely cool, toss in the garlic chips and cilantro and store in an airtight container or tiffin. These last for 3 to 4 weeks for the freshest and most delicious flavor (if you can get them to last that long before eating them by the handful!).

Veggie Manchurian Noodles

⇒⇒ SERVES 2 ⇐⇐

This dish is special to me because it is a rendition of a very popular Indo-Chinese dish called Gobi Manchurian that is an Indo-Chinese staple. *Gobi* means cauliflower in Hindi, and no, Manchurian is not related to the 1959 novel *The Manchurian Candidate* or the 2004 Denzel Washington movie. Manchurian is literally an Indo-Chinese, made-up term to describe this delicious dish, which is most likely based on its origins being from Manchuria . . . or it could be that Indian people just like making names up to make dishes sound tasty. Let's go with the latter. Either way, anything Manchurian-style is scrumptious—it's usually a combination of ginger, garlic, onions, bell peppers, chili-garlic sauce, soy sauce, and fresh cilantro. You really can't go wrong with those flavors!

My Veggie Manchurian Noodles bring together all of those Gobi Manchurian flavors, but without the unhealthy factor of deep-frying the cauliflower. Plus, I make it easy, since all of the elements can be prepped beforehand. And finally, these noodles pack up on-the-go like a charm! So, bring some Manchurian noodles into your life, and leave the candidate on the sidelines, ha!

- 2 tablespoons low-sodium soy sauce
- 1 teaspoon rice wine vinegar
- 1 teaspoon sriracha, sambal, or any red chili sauce
- 1 tablespoon light agave syrup
- 2 teaspoons toasted sesame oil
- 1 tablespoon plus 1 teaspoon neutral oil
- 7 ounces lo mein noodles
- 2 to 3 dried red chilies
- 1 medium yellow onion, thinly sliced
- 3 cloves garlic, minced
- 1 (1-inch) piece fresh ginger, peeled and minced
- 1 red or green bell pepper, thinly sliced
- 1 carrot, peeled and julienned
- 2 tablespoons coarsely chopped fresh cilantro (stems and all!)
- Kosher salt (optional)
- ½ small English cucumber, julienned
- 1 scallion, thinly sliced on the bias
- ⅛ teaspoon black sesame seeds, for garnish
- ⅛ teaspoon white sesame seeds, for garnish

PREPARE THE SAUCE: In a small bowl, mix together the soy sauce, rice wine vinegar, chili sauce, agave, and 1 teaspoon of the sesame oil. Set aside.

COOK THE NOODLES: Place a medium pot filled with water over high heat. Add the 1 teaspoon neutral oil. Once the water comes to a rolling boil, add the lo mein noodles and boil for about 6 minutes, or until tender. Drain, but reserve the cooking water. Tip: to prevent the noodles from sticking together, drizzle the remaining 1 teaspoon sesame oil all over the noodles and toss after boiling. Set aside.

SAUTÉ THE VEGGIES: Place a wok or large nonstick skillet over medium-high heat. Pour in the 1 tablespoon neutral oil. Once it is shimmering and has ripples, the oil is hot! Break the dried red chilies into the hot oil, then add the onion, garlic, and ginger. Sauté for 3 to 4 minutes, until the onion becomes translucent. Add the bell pepper and carrot and sauté for 3 to 4 minutes, until the veggies are slightly fork-tender, but still have a bite.

TIME TO GET SAUCY: Lower the heat to medium-low and pour in the sauce and 2 tablespoons of the reserved cooking water. Simmer, stirring, for 2 to 3 minutes, until bubbling and thicker. Add the noodles and toss to coat completely. If the sauce is getting too thick or not coating all of the noodles, add a bit more reserved cooking water. Toss to coat completely and cook for another 2 to 3 minutes. Toss in 1 tablespoon of the cilantro. Taste to see if it needs salt and add if necessary (it shouldn't need any, though!).

WHAT ABOUT THOSE CUCUMBERS? Place the noodles in your tiffin or serving dish, and top with the cucumber, scallion, remaining 1 tablespoon cilantro, and the sesame seeds. Mix all those goodies in before taking a big bite; enjoy! Tip: if you're on-the-go, drizzle ½ teaspoon toasted sesame oil on top of your noodles before closing the lid of your tiffin. This will help the noodles retain their texture and be a little "slippery" even when consumed at room temperature!

Ginger & Red Pepper Japanese Eggplant

⇒ SERVES 2 ⇐

During one trip to Mumbai, my mom, sisters, and I were hankering for some Indo-Chinese food, because it's the absolute best in Mumbai and we couldn't leave India without getting our fill. Usually I prefer street food stands or local food joints, as I find the food is simply better. However, my father's family chose a fancy hotel restaurant and, I admit, I went in with a negative attitude. But everything turned around once this eggplant dish hit the table—beautiful sautéed eggplant in a ginger-chili sauce and the best, softest, most delicious tofu I had ever eaten. I don't even remember the name of this restaurant (I should probably ask one of my cousins in Mumbai), but I will never forget this dish.

My Ginger & Red Pepper Japanese Eggplant is an ode to that eggplant-tofu dish. Not only is it simple, but it has no garlic *shock face.* Rarely do I cook without garlic, especially in my Indo-Chinese dishes, but the ginger is the star with the eggplant here. It is such a lovely pair—the meatiness of the eggplant complements the earthy spiciness of the ginger. If you are the type that does not like ginger or eggplant (I know there are a few of you out there), I urge you to try this. It brings a whole new perspective to these ingredients, and you may just change your mind—just like I did about fancy restaurants in Mumbai!

2 Japanese eggplants

1 to 2 tablespoons neutral oil

1 teaspoon toasted sesame oil

1 (2-inch) piece fresh ginger, peeled and julienned

1 red jalapeño or Fresno chili pepper, sliced into thin circles

2 scallions, thinly sliced on the bias, white and green parts separated

White pepper

2 teaspoons low-sodium soy sauce

1 teaspoon light agave or raw cane sugar

Kosher salt

½ cup fresh cilantro

1 teaspoon white and black sesame seeds

1½ to 2 cups cooked basmati rice or lo mein noodles, for serving (optional)

CUT THE EGGPLANT: Trim off the stem and cut the eggplant in half horizontally. Slice one of the halves into 4 slices, then cut those slices into ¼- to ½-inch-thick strips. Repeat for the second eggplant.

SAUTÉ TIME: Place a wok or large nonstick skillet over medium-high heat and add 1 tablespoon of the neutral oil. Once the oil is hot, add the sesame oil and eggplant strips. Toss to coat the eggplant completely with the oil and ensure that most (if not all) the eggplant strips are touching the hot skillet. Use tongs to move the strips around constantly. After about 2 minutes, toss in the ginger, jalapeño, and white parts of the scallions. The eggplant should be getting soft and browned. Add a pinch of pepper and, if the skillet seems to be drying up, add up to another tablespoon of neutral oil—eggplant has the tendency to absorb a lot of oil! Once the eggplant is fork-tender, after 8 to 10 minutes, add the soy sauce and agave and toss to coat completely. Give it a quick taste and add some salt if necessary.

FINISH AND GARNISH: Slightly trim the edges off the cilantro, but not the whole stem. Then cut the cilantro into four parts, rather than chopping it. Add to the eggplant and toss. Remove the eggplant from the heat and garnish with the sesame seeds and green parts of the scallions. Serve with rice, noodles, or even on its own. If traveling and pairing with rice or noodles, pack the carb on the bottom of the tiffin first, then top with the Ginger & Red Pepper Japanese Eggplant. Enjoy!

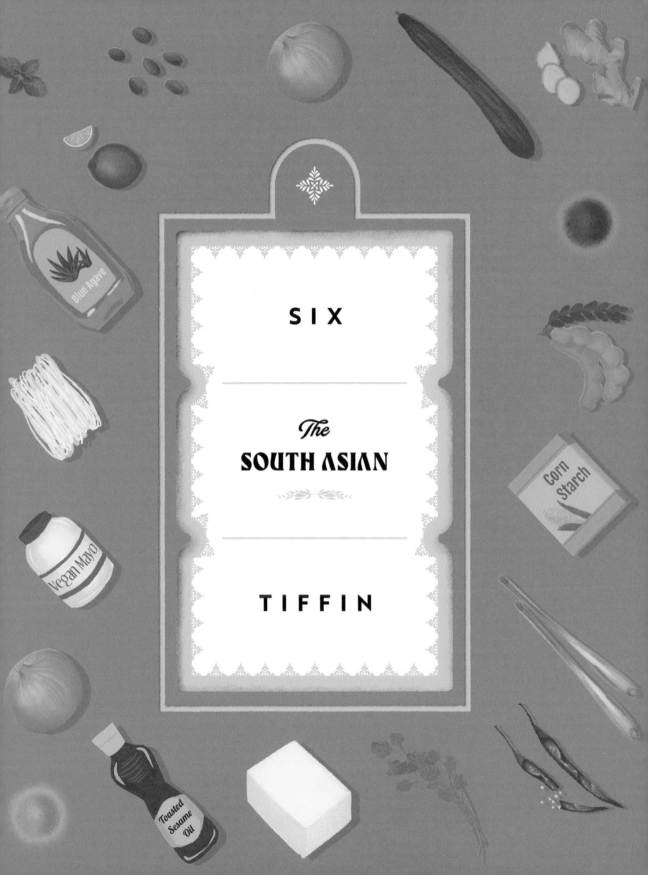

SIX

The
SOUTH ASIAN

TIFFIN

This is an interesting chapter that I thought really long and hard on what to name. As someone who's from a culture that was generally overlooked in the States until recently, and has been "bucketed" into the broad category "Asian," I am sensitive to titles. But I landed on South Asian, because this chapter is truly a compilation of recipes from various South Asian countries: Thailand, Vietnam, and Indonesia (by way of Belize, as you'll see!). There are still many places within the South Asian region where I wish to travel, but I have tasted quite a large amount through travels to Thailand, Australia, Belize, and New York City, which has some very delicious Vietnamese and Thai restaurants! You're probably thinking right about now, "Um, Priyanka, Belize is nowhere near South Asia. Do you need a geography lesson?" You're going to have to wait for the last recipe in this chapter to understand how and why Belize comes into the picture. It just goes to show how much smaller the world really is than we think!

In any case, I love these recipes—they all have bold flavors, a variation of textures and temperatures, and are fun to eat. 'Cause eating *should* be fun, right? And as with most of the recipes in this book, some of these recipes are inspired by my travels and by some of my favorites eats in the States. Come to think of it, I may have a subconscious obsession with Vietnamese food from being exposed to the musical *Miss Saigon* when I was a child, since my sisters performed in it and constantly played and sang the songs at home. But, it's just a theory after all!

Vietnamese-Style Vermicelli Noodle Salad

⇒ SERVES 2 ⇐

Cold noodles, anyone? Sounds kind of odd, I know, but so smart if you think about it! They can be made ahead of time, don't require to be heated up, and taste better the longer they sit. Sounds like the perfect kind of dish to me! I've eaten all variations of cold noodles—within Sichuan-style Chinese cuisine, Thai cuisine, and Vietnamese cuisine. And I would have to say the Vietnamese cold noodles were my favorite. From my experience, they're generally made with a glass or mung bean noodle, tossed with a bunch of cool, crispy veggies, and served with an extra spicy red chili and buttery peanut sauce. Basically, all of my favorite things in one place—variation of textures, spicy, slightly sweet, and filled with the colors of the rainbow. My Vietnamese-Style Vermicelli Noodle Salad encompasses all of those attributes but has a little Indian twist with the addition of turmeric—we can always use a little immune boost or two! This dish is absolutely perfect for meal prep, picnics, road trips, or just a simple lunch at home.

TURMERIC-SESAME DRESSING

- 1 stalk fresh lemongrass
- ½ cup fresh orange juice
- ½ teaspoon turmeric powder
- 1 (1-inch) piece fresh ginger, with peel on
- 2 cloves garlic, peeled and slightly smashed
- 1 dried red chili
- 1 teaspoon toasted sesame oil
- 2 teaspoons light agave
- 1 teaspoon cornstarch
- Pinch of kosher salt, plus more for seasoning
- Pinch of freshly ground black pepper
- ¼ teaspoon white sesame seeds

- 4 ounces vermicelli noodles
- 1 carrot
- ½ English cucumber
- 2 teaspoons toasted sesame oil
- 1 bunch baby bok choy
- 2 tablespoons coarsely chopped unsalted dry-roasted peanuts, lightly toasted

GARNISHES

- 2 tablespoons coarsely chopped fresh cilantro (stems and all!)
- 2 sprigs fresh mint leaves, coarsely chopped
- 1 scallion, thinly sliced on the bias, white and green parts separated
- 2 tablespoons unsalted dry-roasted peanuts, ground in a mortar and pestle
- ½ teaspoon white sesame seeds, lightly toasted
- 2 wedges lime

Method follows

MAKE THE DRESSING: Place the lemongrass on a cutting board. Using the back of your knife or the pestle from a mortar, smash the lemongrass throughout to break up slightly. This will release the aroma and juices within. Cut into quarters and place in a small pot. Add the orange juice, turmeric, ginger, garlic, red chili, the 1 teaspoon oil, and the agave. Place over medium-low heat and bring to a simmer. Make a cornstarch slurry in a separate small bowl, mixing together the cornstarch with 1 tablespoon water until smooth with no visible lumps. The orange juice mixture should be simmering and very aromatic after 3 to 4 minutes. Stir in the cornstarch slurry. Add the salt and pepper and simmer for another 3 to 4 minutes for the sauce to thicken—it should become the texture of a thin maple syrup. Give it a taste—it should be tangy, spicy, fresh, and slightly sweet. Add more salt if necessary. Add the sesame seeds right at the end. Remove from the heat and let cool. Using tongs, remove the garlic, ginger, whole red chili, and lemongrass. Chop the garlic, remove the peel from the ginger and chop, and break up the chili. Set aside. Discard the lemongrass.

PREP THE VERMICELLI AND VEGGIES: Fill a medium pot with water and bring to a boil. Once the water is boiling, remove from the stove, add the vermicelli noodles, and soak for 5 to 6 minutes, until tender. Drain and set aside. Using a vegetable peeler, peel the outer layer of the carrot and save to use for a vegetable stock. Continue peeling the carrot to create thin ribbons. Use the same method on the English cucumber but keeping the peel. Set the ribbons aside.

SAUTÉ: In a large nonstick skillet, heat the 2 teaspoons sesame oil over medium-high heat. Add the reserved chopped garlic, ginger, and chili and sauté for 30 seconds. Add the boy choy and sauté for 3 to 4 minutes, until the green tops are slightly wilted and the white bottoms are fork-tender. Transfer to a large bowl.

ASSEMBLE: Add the cooked vermicelli, carrot and cucumber ribbons, chopped peanuts, and cooled dressing. Using tongs, toss everything together until well coated. Then add 1 tablespoon each of cilantro, mint, and the white parts of the scallion. Toss again, making sure everything is incorporated well together and is nicely coated. Give it a taste! It should be savory, sweet, tangy, and spicy. Place into the tiffin or on a serving platter. Garnish with the peanuts, remaining cilantro, mint, green parts of the scallion, the sesame seeds, and lime wedges. Serve with chopsticks. If traveling, simply place your Vietnamese-Style Vermicelli Noodle Salad into your tiffin and eat at your destination at room temperature.

Tofu Bánh Mì

⁂ SERVES 2 ⁂

Please tell me you've eaten a bánh mì before. If you have not, then you're missing out on one of the great sandwiches born from not-so-great colonization. Yes, that's right. Have you ever noticed that bánh mì is made with a loaf of French bread? And have you ever wondered, why is a Vietnamese sandwich made with French bread? Well, I did, which led me to doing my research. Bánh mì is from the French colonization era of Vietnam, when the French introduced baguettes, and the rest is history. Traditionally, bánh mì is made with marinated pork or chicken and topped with a tangy slaw, spicy jalapeños, red chili spread, and tons of fresh cilantro. My Tofu Bánh Mì is made with a tamarind-marinated tofu, spicy and tangy slaw, and tons of jalapeños and fresh cilantro. Your next question might be, "Priyanka, why are you obsessed with bánh mì if you haven't even been to Vietnam?" Thanks to a little restaurant in the West Village of Manhattan called Saigon Shack, I've been eating these delicious sandwiches for years. Every component of the sandwich is important and cannot go overlooked. So, my advice here is: don't skimp on the bread. If you can find a *good* and fresh French baguette, grab it!

TOFU MARINADE

- 8 ounces extra-firm tofu, drained
- ½ cup low-sodium soy sauce
- 1 tablespoon rice wine vinegar
- 1 (1-inch) piece fresh ginger, peeled and grated
- 2 cloves garlic, grated
- 1 tablespoon toasted sesame oil
- 1 teaspoon white sesame seeds
- 2 dried red chilies
- 2 tablespoons light agave
- Juice from ½ lime
- 1 heaping tablespoon tamarind chutney (see Note)

BÁNH MÌ SLAW

- 1 carrot, julienned
- ½ English cucumber, julienned
- 1 jalapeño, thinly sliced into circles
- ½ bunch fresh cilantro, coarsely chopped (stems and all!)
- 1 tablespoon light agave
- 5 sprigs fresh mint, cut into chiffonade
- ¼ cup reserved tofu marinade
- Zest from ½ lime

SPICY SPREAD

- ¼ cup vegan mayonnaise
- 2 tablespoons sriracha

- 1 teaspoon neutral oil
- ½ fresh loaf French baguette, sliced in half horizontally to make 2 individual loaves

Method follows

PRESS AND CUT THE TOFU: In order to achieve a flavorful and intact tofu "steak" for our bánh mì, we need to press out all the moisture. Wrap the tofu block in a thick kitchen towel and place it onto a plate. Place a heavy mortar and pestle or heavy pan on top of it. Place the whole contraption in the sink, so any excess moisture can drain out directly into the sink. Let the tofu drain for at least 10 to 15 minutes. Carefully remove the pan/mortar and pestle and uncover the tofu from the towel. It should look a bit drier and still be intact. Place onto a cutting board. Slice the tofu into 4 even slices lengthwise. Set aside.

MAKE THE MARINADE: In a large shallow bowl, mix together all of the ingredients for the marinade except for the tofu. Give it a taste—it should be spicy, tangy, slightly salty, and fairly thin in consistency. Place the pressed tofu slabs into the marinade and gently turn so they are covered on all sides. Marinate for 10 minutes.

MEANWHILE, MAKE THE SLAW: In a large bowl, toss together the reserved tofu marinade with all of the ingredients—using only half of the cilantro, reserving the remainder for garnish. Toss until well coated.

MAKE THE SPICY SPREAD: In a small bowl, mix together the vegan mayonnaise and sriracha. The color should be light red, and it should taste spicy!

SEAR THE TOFU: Heat a large nonstick skillet over medium-high heat. Add the neutral oil. Once it's hot, using the tongs, lift up each piece of tofu and place it into the skillet. It should sizzle. Sear on each side for 4 to 5 minutes, until charred on the edges and medium brown in the center. Repeat until all tofu "steaks" are cooked. Set aside. Slice each loaf of bread in half lengthwise and place inside-down onto the same skillet to toast for 2 to 3 minutes, until golden brown and slightly crisp. Remove and place onto a cutting board.

ASSEMBLY TIME: Spread a heaping tablespoon of spicy spread onto each bottom half of the loaf, top with two tofu steaks, pile on the slaw, and garnish with the remaining cilantro. Close and eat immediately or pack in your tiffin. If doing so, the spread will slightly soften the bread, but won't make it soggy since we used a crusty French loaf!

✕ ——————————————————————————

NOTE: See the Glossary (page 194) on buying the best store-bought chutneys and some of my favorite brands.

Bangkok-inspired Street Noodles

SERVES 2

You are probably not hearing it here first, but the street food in Thailand is next level. Specifically, in Bangkok. The streets are filled with all sorts of street food carts with all sorts of dishes. Unfortunately (and to no surprise), I couldn't consume much of it. I obviously do not speak Thai, so it was difficult for me to confirm which dishes were completely meat-free. But, after some help from the locals and some research, I was able to learn some key words— "no meat" and "extra spicy," obviously the only words I needed to know. Then finally I was able to eat a few things. One dish in particular that I saw pop up around Bangkok was flash-fried noodles with greens—but not any ordinary greens, romaine lettuce to be exact! Yes, lettuce is sautéed with the noodle dishes and it is absolutely mind-blowing! Not wilting or gross, definitely not the sad lettuce sitting in the back of your fridge crying, no! But crisp and fresh, adding the perfect cooling touch to the spicy noodles. I loved this concept, not only because I learned something, but it also gave a whole new life to a vegetable that I had only thought of using in one way.

My Bangkok-inspired Street Noodles are a rendition of what I ate on the streets of Bangkok, but with an added healthy twist—I've made this with bean noodles, so we can pack in the protein and not the carbs! But this dish can be easily made with rice noodles or lo mein. Any noodle works! So, lettuce (see what I did there?) grow together and continue expanding our perspectives on foods and vegetables that we may *think* we know!

4 ounces edamame or adzuki bean spaghetti

1 teaspoon toasted sesame oil

1 tablespoon neutral oil

2 to 3 dried red chilies, broken in half

¼ cup unsalted dry-roasted peanuts plus 1 tablespoon ground peanuts

1 medium yellow onion, thinly sliced

4 cloves garlic, thinly sliced

1 (1-inch) piece fresh ginger, peeled and minced

Pinch of kosher salt

10 to 12 leaves romaine lettuce, broken in half and ends trimmed off, plus extra for garnish

½ cup grape tomatoes, sliced in half lengthwise

2 to 3 tablespoons low-sodium soy sauce, or to taste

Kosher salt (optional)

BOIL THE NOODLES: Place a large pot of water over high heat and bring to a boil. Add the bean noodles and boil for about 5 minutes, until al dente. Drain and add the sesame oil and toss; this will keep the noodles from clumping together. Set aside.

SAUTÉ TIME: Place a large nonstick skillet over medium-high heat and pour in the neutral oil. Once the oil has ripples, it's hot! Add the chilies and the ¼ cup dry-roasted peanuts and sauté for 30 seconds. Add the onion, garlic, ginger, and salt. Sauté for about 5 minutes, until the onion is sweating and is slightly golden. Add the romaine lettuce and toss. Once the lettuce begins to wilt, after about 1 minute, add the tomatoes. Once the tomatoes are slightly blistered, after about a minute and a half, add the noodles, breaking them up with your hands so they don't clump, and the soy sauce and toss. Make sure that everything gets coated and incorporated together. Give it a quick taste and add salt if necessary.

GARNISH AND SERVE: Place the extra romaine leaves on a serving dish and, using tongs, place the noodles on top of the lettuce and garnish with the 1 tablespoon ground peanuts. If traveling, layer the lettuce leaves on the bottom of your tiffin and top with the noodles and ground peanuts. The lettuce will have slightly wilted upon eating at your destination, but that is exactly how we like it. Enjoy!

Peanut Sauce Dressing

⇶ MAKES ABOUT 1 CUP ⇷

Ever since I was a child, I've always ordered extra peanut sauce at any Thai, Vietnamese, or South Asian restaurant. To me, it was a "pour over or dunk everything into" sauce. There is something about a good peanut sauce that I love. Perhaps it's the fact that I love anything peanut-based, or that a well-made peanut sauce has the perfect balance of tang, sweet, spice, and butteriness? And let me tell you, when I traveled to Thailand in 2016, I got my hands on whatever peanut sauce I could find! Aside from the fact that the ingredients themselves tasted better in Thailand than they do in the States (the red chili is spicier, the peanuts have a stronger peanut flavor, the sugar is sweeter), I wasn't going to leave the source of peanut sauce without eating so much that I got sick of it. Shocker: I did not get sick, or tired, of eating peanut sauce on the daily. My Peanut Sauce Dressing is a little gateway to my peanut sauce obsession. I add a little Kashmiri chili powder for a beautiful color and some turmeric, because I love its earthy flavor in combination with the spice and tang of the dressing. I hope my Peanut Sauce Dressing makes you just as obsessed with peanut sauce as I am!

TOAST THE NUTS: In a medium nonstick skillet, add the peanuts and dried chili. Toast over medium heat for 2 to 3 minutes, until there is a little color on the peanuts. Transfer to a food processor or blender. Begin to blend on high until the peanuts break down and start to resemble a peanut butter consistency. Give the food processor a break in between to regain energy! Once it's a smooth peanut butter consistency, add the cilantro and blend until it's finely chopped into the peanut butter mixture. Transfer to a bowl.

LET'S MAKE IT SAUCY: Add all the remaining ingredients and whisk together. If the mixture is too thick, add 2 tablespoons warm water and continue whisking. I prefer a thicker peanut sauce, but if you would like it thinner, add up to 2 more tablespoons warm water. Give it a taste—it should be nutty, spicy, tangy, and savory. If you feel that it is missing salt, add a splash more soy sauce.

STORE: Transfer to an airtight container or mason jar and store in the pantry or fridge for up to 3 to 4 weeks. If storing in the fridge, allow the peanut sauce to come to room temperature before serving or eating, which makes this absolutely perfect for traveling! Drizzle on pretty much anything.

1 cup unsalted dry-roasted peanuts

1 dried red chili

2 tablespoons coarsely chopped fresh cilantro (stems and all!)

⅛ teaspoon Kashmiri chili powder

¼ teaspoon turmeric powder

2 teaspoons rice wine vinegar

1 tablespoon light agave

Juice from ½ lime

2 tablespoons low-sodium soy sauce

Toasted Coconut Chili Peanuts

⇒⫸ SERVES 2 ⫷⇐

You've arrived at the recipe in this chapter that I've been hinting at! The recipe that originates from a country that is not anywhere near South Asia, but has some surprising ties—Belize! I had the opportunity to visit Belize in 2019 with my family and learned so much. Yes, Belize is technically part of Central America, is attached to the peninsula of Mexico, and neighbors Guatemala. But what is fascinating about Belize is that it is comprised of multiple cultures through colonizations of the past. Some of the main cultures and backgrounds include Mestizo, Mayan, Creole, East Indian, various European, and Asian. So, to be Belizean means that you're actually very much mixed, and I find that to be the coolest thing ever!

While I was there, I had the great opportunity one evening to cook alongside the executive chef of Turtle Inn (a Coppola-owned property) to make a full feast. And that is when I learned about this coconut-chili peanut dish. It tasted surprisingly Asian—a cross between Thai and Vietnamese, in my opinion. I asked the chef, what is this dish and why does it taste Asian? He explained that there is a large amount of South Asian, specifically Indonesian and Polynesian, influence in Belize, which manifests itself in the food. And I thought that was the coolest thing ever.

Out of everything we cooked together, this peanut dish was likely the simplest, but the tastiest! It was sweet, slightly smoky, spicy, and crunchy. Once again, I was shown that the world is so much smaller than we think! I hope my Toasted Coconut Chili Peanuts transport you to Bali by way of Belize—either way, you'll be transported to a beautiful destination.

1 dried red chili

1 red jalapeño or Fresno chili pepper

2 cloves garlic, peeled

2 teaspoons rice wine vinegar

1 teaspoon light agave

Pinch of kosher salt

½ cup grated fresh coconut

½ cup unsalted dry-roasted peanuts

PREPARE AHEAD: Soak the dried red chili in warm water for at least 2 hours—this will help soften the chili, making it easier to blend. Meanwhile, remove the stem from the jalapeño and coarsely chop. Once the dried chili is soaked, add all the chilies to a blender with the garlic, rice wine vinegar, agave, and salt. Blend until the mixture becomes a chunky paste. If it's too thick, add in a tablespoon of the chili soaking water. This will be very spicy.

TOAST THE COCONUT AND PEANUTS: In a medium nonstick skillet, toast the coconut over medium-low heat for about 4 minutes, until slightly golden and slightly crisp. Add the peanuts and toast for 3 to 4 minutes, until the coconut is more golden and the peanuts are slightly browned. Add the garlic-chili sauce and toss to coat. Let the mixture heat through completely for 2 minutes. Transfer to a shallow bowl or tiffin. Let cool before serving. This tastes best at room temperature. It keeps well in the pantry in an airtight container for about 1 week.

SEVEN

The
MEXICAN
TIFFIN

I've always said that in some alternate universe, Mexico and India were attached as countries. Even thinking back to Pangea, Mexico and India did not touch in any way—they were at opposite ends—which is why I say in an "alternate universe." There is so much overlap in food and culture, at least in my opinion! Our staple ingredients are quite similar— fresh cilantro, citrus (lime/lemon), chilies, cumin, and a variety of textures. Indian and Mexican cultures are incredibly colorful, and the colors have a lot of meaning within tradition; there is utmost respect for ancestry and respecting elders; and believing that there is a life after death (whether it's Día de los Muertos or the Hindu concept of reincarnation). This probably explains why Indians love Mexican food—okay, I can only speak on behalf of Indians within the States—but I guarantee you will not meet an Indian person in the States who dislikes Mexican food. Heck, our favorite place to dine out is Taco Bell! (Put your judgment away, because Taco Bell was the only quick-service restaurant that included vegetarian and vegan options before veganism was a trend. And it's delicious. But I digress.)

Needless to say, my family and I love Mexican food, and that led us to travel to Mexico quite a bit. I've ventured around Cabo San Lucas, Cancún, Riviera Maya, and one of the best foodie cities in the world—La Ciudad de México. And I loved every bite! Not to mention, there is SO much to eat for vegetarians and vegans! My Mexican Tiffin chapter is inspired by my delicious experiences eating around Mexico and New York City. You may find some unusual combinations, but I assure you, they're delicious. Just go in with an open mind, kick up your spice tolerance a bit, and get those elastic pants on!

Mango Gazpacho

⇒⅞ SERVES 2 ⅝⇐

Yes, I understand this is the Mexican Tiffin chapter and not the Spanish Tiffin chapter, so why is there a gazpacho, you ask? Well, this isn't a typical Spanish gazpacho—this combines the elements of a traditional gazpacho (a cool and chunky soup) with the concept of Indian mango pulp (fresh mango ground down to a pulp and mixed with sugar and cardamom), but with Mexican ingredients. I told you at the start of this book that things may get weird. And they certainly have. I love this recipe, not only because it combines all those cultures, but because it takes me back to La Coyoacán, outside of Frida Kahlo's house, where I bought a whole ripe mango covered in red chili powder from a street cart. A sweet and spicy delight! This Mango Gazpacho is just that. Ripe and juicy mangoes combined with spicy habanero, lime, and fresh summer veggies. It's time to slurp up some gazpacho, so get your bib on!

2 ripe mangoes, preferably Kent mangoes

¼ teaspoon cumin seeds

1 habanero or serrano chili pepper

½ English cucumber, diced

1 small red bell pepper, diced

Fresh lime zest from ½ lime

Fresh juice from ½ lime

¼ teaspoon kosher salt, plus more for seasoning

Pinch of freshly ground black pepper

2 scallions, sliced on the diagonal, white and green parts separated

¼ cup coarsely chopped fresh cilantro (stems and all!)

Olive oil, for drizzling

CUT THE MANGOES: Using a sharp chef's knife, trim off the top of the mango where the cavity is. Place the flat side of the mango on a cutting board. The large pit is in the middle of the mango, so gently cut lengthwise down one side around the pit to reveal one half. Repeat on the other side to reveal the second side. Cut the remaining thin sides until you're left with just the pit. Squeeze the flesh of the mango from the skin into a large bowl. Use a teaspoon to scoop out any remaining flesh. Repeat with the second mango. Using your hand (or a potato masher), mash the mango until all the fibers are broken down and the texture becomes homogenous.

PREP THE SPICES: Preheat an oven or toaster oven to 375°F. Toast the cumin seeds in a small skillet over medium heat for 1 minute until fragrant. Pour into a mortar and pestle and grind coarsely. Set aside. Now, time for the habanero. Put on disposable gloves and place the whole habanero on a cookie sheet and roast for 10 minutes, turning once, until slightly charred on all sides. Using tongs, place the habanero on a cutting board to completely cool. Cut in half, remove the stem and seeds, and discard them. Mince the habanero and add to the mango puree. Remove and discard the gloves and thoroughly wash your hands.

LET'S MAKE GAZPACHO: To the mango-habanero puree, add the cumin, cucumber, bell pepper, lime zest, lime juice, salt, black pepper, white parts of the scallions, and half of the cilantro. Stir until well combined. Give it a taste—it should be spicy, slightly sweet, tangy, and slightly smoky. Add more salt if necessary.

GARNISH AND SERVE: If eating immediately, pour into two shallow bowls, drizzle each with oil, and top with the green parts of the scallions and the remaining cilantro. If traveling, place the Mango Gazpacho in your tiffin and drizzle with oil. Pack up the fresh cilantro and scallions separately and garnish before eating; enjoy!

Masala Esquites

⋙ SERVES 2 ⋘

You must've heard about esquites by now. No? Well, it's fresh corn roasted on the cob, then sheared off and mixed with a creamy mayonnaise mixture, chili pepper, and a generous amount of cotija cheese. I'm not going to lie—it's darn good. And funny enough, there is a slightly similar street corn dish in India referred to as masala corn or corn chaat—mixed with chutneys, fresh cilantro, spices, the works! I already told you at the start of this chapter that I am convinced that Mexico and India were attached as countries in some alternate universe. My Masala Esquites brings that theory to life, as it combines the concept of Mexican esquites with Indian flavors. This dish is perfect as a side, an appetizer, or even a lunch. Did I mention this would go fabulously in a grilled sandwich, wrapped in a burrito, or even on top of a pizza? Yum!

2 ears corn

⅛ teaspoon cumin seeds

⅛ teaspoon coriander seeds

1 dried red chili

1 heaping tablespoon vegan mayonnaise

½ fresh lime plus 2 wedges, for garnish

1 clove garlic, grated

2 heaping tablespoons coarsely chopped fresh cilantro (stems and all!)

2 pinches kosher salt

1 tablespoon unsalted raw almonds

Pinch of chaat masala (optional)

CHAR THE CORN: Peel off all the husk and silk from the corn but keep the stem on. Using tongs, hold the corn over a medium-low open flame on the stove. The flame will begin to char the corn—be careful, as this will pop. Keep turning the corn around to char all sides evenly. Once the corn is charred and slightly blackened all around, remove and let cool on a cutting board. Repeat with the second ear of corn.

LET'S GET SPICY: Place a small skillet over medium-low heat. Add the cumin seeds, coriander seeds, and red chili. Toast for 1 to 2 minutes, until fragrant and the chili is slightly charred. Transfer to a mortar and pestle. Grind as fine as you can. Set aside.

MAKE THE DRESSING: In a medium bowl, add the mayonnaise, ground spice mix, lime juice, garlic, 1 tablespoon of the cilantro, and a pinch of salt. Stir until everything is incorporated and smooth.

CUT THE CORN: Place a kitchen towel on the cutting board and hold the charred corn by the stem upright on the kitchen towel. Using a sharp chef's knife or serrated knife, carefully slice down the sides of the cob to release all the kernels. Repeat until both cobs are sheared.

TIME TO GET MIXIN': Add the charred corn kernels to the mayonnaise mixture and toss to completely coat. Taste, but don't add any more salt, as the chaat masala is salty and we will be using that as a garnish!

WHAT ABOUT THE COTIJA CHEESE? Place the almonds in a food processor. Pulse until you have a coarsely ground texture—almost similar to a Parmesan. Transfer to a small bowl. Add a pinch of salt and toss.

GARNISH AND SERVE: Place the Masala Esquites in a serving dish or into your tiffin if traveling. Top with the almond "cotija" cheese, a pinch of chaat masala, if using, and the remaining cilantro, and serve with the lime wedges. The longer this sits, the more flavorful it gets—and this is meant to be eaten at room temperature, so it's perfect for traveling!

Chipotle Black Bean & Corn Tostada

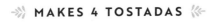 MAKES 4 TOSTADAS

One of the fondest food memories I have of traveling in Mexico is ditching a day trip to explore Ciudad Prehispánica de Teotihuacán and, instead, spending a day in the city to stuff my face and take a mezcal tour. Best choice of my life at the time, because that day I tasted some of the best Mexican food ever. The *mercados* in Mexico, specifically in La Ciudad de México, are extensive, filled with tons of produce, snacks, dried fruits, and food stalls. My friend Jenn and I sat down at one of the tostada stands in the middle of the market—it wasn't too crowded or busy, so we initially had mixed feelings. We placed our order, and the cooks made it right in front of us— a freshly fried, crisp flour tortilla topped with black beans, veggies, tons of iceberg lettuce, crema, and avocado, served with four different spicy salsas. One bite and I knew that this was one of the best meals I would ever have. It was so simple yet complex—crispy tortilla, soft veggies, cool lettuce, spicy salsa; it was seriously an explosion of flavors in my mouth! So that is exactly what I wanted to emulate in my Chipotle Black Bean & Corn Tostada: a variation of textures, spices, and temperatures. If you don't fall in love with this dish, then I'm convinced you're not a foodie.

4 corn tortillas

2 teaspoons neutral oil, plus more for frying

2 cloves garlic, minced

1 jalapeño, diced (seeds and all!)

1 (15-ounce) can black beans, rinsed and drained

½ cup canned or frozen corn kernels

Pinch of kosher salt

Pinch of freshly ground black pepper

Fresh juice from ½ lime

CHIPOTLE CREMA

¼ heaping cup nondairy sour cream

2 chipotle peppers in adobo plus 1 tablespoon adobo sauce

1 heaping tablespoon coarsely chopped fresh cilantro (stems and all!)

⅛ teaspoon cumin seeds

Pinch of kosher salt, plus more for seasoning

Pinch of freshly ground black pepper

GARNISHES

1 cup iceberg lettuce, shredded

¼ cup vegan feta cheese, crumbled

½ Hass avocado, thinly sliced

1 red radish, thinly sliced

3 tablespoons fresh cilantro leaves

Method follows

CRISP THE TORTILLAS: Pour a shallow layer, about 1 inch, of oil into a heavy-bottom pan and set over medium-high heat. Give the oil 1 to 2 minutes to heat up. Meanwhile, prick the tortillas all over with a fork, which will prevent air bubbles from forming. Once the oil is shimmering and has ripples, it's ready to go! Add 1 tortilla—it should sizzle—and press it down with tongs to ensure it stays flat. After about 1 minute, flip, and it should be golden. Cook the other side for another 1 to 2 minutes, until golden. Using tongs, carefully transfer to a paper towel–lined plate to drain the oil. Let cool and repeat with the other tortillas.

SAUTÉ THE VEGGIES: In a medium nonstick skillet, add the 2 teaspoons oil and place over medium heat. Once the oil heats up, add the garlic and jalapeños and sauté for 1 minute. Add the black beans and corn. Sprinkle in the salt and black pepper and cook for 6 to 8 minutes, until the beans are soft enough to be gently crushed with the back of a spoon. Squeeze in the lime juice right at the end, toss, and remove from the heat.

MAKE THE CHIPOTLE CREMA: Place all of the ingredients in a blender and blend until very smooth. Taste and add more salt if necessary. The texture should be creamy, but not thick like a paste, and light red. Pour into a squeezy bottle and set aside.

ASSEMBLE THE TOSTADAS: Layer the tortillas on a platter and top each with a heaping spoonful of the black bean–corn mixture. Squeeze the chipotle crema all over, then top with a handful of iceberg lettuce, feta, a few slices of avocado, slices of radish, and cilantro. If traveling, pack the tortillas in one tiffin, the black bean mixture in another tiffin, and the garnishes together in a third tiffin, leaving the seed in the avocado to prevent it from oxidizing. Bring the crema in the squeezy bottle.

Green Chutney Quesadillas

MAKES 2 LARGE QUESADILLAS

One can never go wrong with a quesadilla—two tortillas grilled together with gooey cheese in between? I mean, come on! Just writing that has got me hungry! But have you ever tried chutney with a quesadilla? I'm not going to lie, this recipe is inspired by two things: the street-side quesadillas that I ate in La Ciudad de México, fresh off the grill made with hand-rolled blue corn tortillas and topped with salsa verde and . . . wait for it . . . my lazy lunches at home. Many-a-times, on a busy working day (which is every day for me), my quick-fix lunch is a quesadilla filled with gooey vegan Monterey Jack cheese paired with an Indian green chutney. Yup! And it is *so* good. If you've never tried this before, you're in luck—this Green Chutney Quesadilla combines all those goodies and may even transport you to the festive and delicious streets of México!

GREEN CHUTNEY

- ¼ cup coarsely chopped fresh cilantro (stems and all!)
- 2 cloves garlic, coarsely chopped
- 1 (¼-inch) piece fresh ginger, peeled
- 1 serrano chili pepper
- Pinch of kosher salt

- 3 teaspoons olive oil
- 1 small sweet potato, peeled and sliced lengthwise
- 1 medium yellow onion, sliced
- 1 large red bell pepper, julienned
- Pinch of kosher salt
- 2 jumbo flour tortillas
- 6 slices vegan mozzarella or white American cheese
- Fresh cilantro leaves, for garnish
- 2 lime wedges, for serving

CREAMY CUMIN SAUCE

- ¼ heaping cup nondairy sour cream
- 2 to 3 tablespoons unsweetened nondairy creamer
- ¼ teaspoon cumin seeds
- 1 teaspoon fresh lime juice
- ¼ teaspoon fresh lime zest
- Pinch of ground cinnamon
- Pinch of kosher salt, plus more for seasoning
- Pinch of freshly ground black pepper

MAKE THE GREEN CHUTNEY: In a food processor or blender, add the cilantro, garlic, ginger, serrano, and salt. Washing the cilantro right before blending is key, so the moisture can help the blending process. Start blending—if you have trouble, add a tablespoon of water. Continue blending until smooth. Set aside. Rinse down the food processor or blender.

SAUTÉ THE VEGGIES: The veggies should be cut in similar sizes to strive for even and consistent cooking. Place a large nonstick skillet over medium-high heat. Add 2 teaspoons of the oil. Once the oil is shimmering and has ripples, it's hot! Add the sweet potatoes and sauté, using tongs to consistently toss so all sides are hitting the hot skillet, for 3 to 4 minutes, until the sweet potatoes start to color. Add the onion, bell pepper, and salt, lower the heat to medium-low, and cook for another 10 minutes or so, until the sweet potato is fork-tender and the onion has sweated and is slightly caramelized. Add the Green Chutney and toss until coated. Transfer to a plate or bowl and set aside.

MAKE THE CREAMY CUMIN SAUCE: In the food processor or blender, blend together all of the ingredients until very smooth with no visible lumps. Taste and add salt if necessary.

QUESADILLA TIME: Wipe down the large skillet and set over medium heat. Add the remaining 1 teaspoon oil and spread around with a spatula. Add 1 tortilla and layer on 2 slices of cheese to one side of the tortilla and 1 slice to the other side. Add the green chutney veggies on the side with 2 slices of cheese and carefully close the quesadilla to a half-moon shape. Press down with the spatula and sear for 2 minutes until golden, then carefully flip and cook another 2 minutes until golden. Slide onto a cutting board. Repeat with the second tortilla. Cut the quesadillas into wedges, garnish with the cilantro, and serve with the cumin dip and lime wedges. If traveling, place the cut quesadilla wedges into your tiffin with the lime wedges and pack the cumin dip separately. Dunk on arrival!

Poblano Torta

MAKES 2 TORTAS

One hot afternoon in La Ciudad de México, I was meant to visit one of the most highly regarded museums in all of Mexico, the National Museum of Anthropology, but I quickly became distracted by some delicious grilled cactus sandwiches outside the museum. It was the whiff that really drew me in—the smell of charred vegetables, toasted bread, and melted cheese—and the fact that anything being cooked on the side of a street is immediately appealing to me. So, I had to stop and take a look—and I was so happy to see that vegetarian sandwiches were being made on a separate griddle from the meat one! Thinly sliced *nopales* (cactus) charred on a hot griddle and piled high on a *bolillo* (crusty Mexican bread) with tons of oil and spicy salsa. Needless to say, I immediately bought one, awkwardly videotaped the whole cooking process, and stuffed my face without sharing ('cause why would I share? It's mine, duh). And let me tell you—it was heavenly.

The process? They press together the sandwich under a cast-iron block, so everything melts together and just tastes like spicy sandwich heaven. When the cactus is charred, it has a similar texture to poblanos, which I love! My Poblano Torta is inspired by this delicious nopales torta I ate in front of a museum instead of becoming a more artistic and worldly individual. Well worth it if you ask me!

2 poblano peppers

⅛ teaspoon cumin seeds

3 to 4 dried pequin chili peppers (see Note)

2 teaspoons neutral oil

1 medium yellow onion, sliced in half and thinly sliced lengthwise

Pinch of kosher salt

Pinch of freshly ground black pepper

Juice from ½ lime

2 crusty rolls, such as bolillo or French rolls

4 to 6 romaine lettuce leaves, broken in half

4 slices beefsteak tomato

4 slices vegan Monterey Jack, mozzarella, or white American cheese

LIME AIOLI

4 tablespoons vegan mayonnaise

Zest from ½ lime

Juice from ½ lime

⅛ teaspoon cumin powder

⅛ teaspoon raw cane sugar

Pinch of freshly ground black pepper

1 tablespoon fresh cilantro leaves

PREPARE THE VEGGIES: Slice the poblano peppers in half and remove the stem and seeds. Lay each half skin side down on a cutting board and cut into quarters lengthwise; you should have 8 slices of poblano in total. Coarsely grind the cumin seeds and pequin pepper in a mortar and pestle. Be careful, as the pequin peppers are spicy—do not rub your eyes, and wash your hands immediately after. Next, heat a large nonstick skillet over medium-high heat and pour in the oil to coat the skillet. Once the oil is hot, add the ground spices and toss in the oil for 30 seconds, then add the onion. Sauté until the onion begins to sweat and becomes translucent, about 4 minutes. Slightly lower the heat and add the sliced poblanos, salt, and black pepper. Toss in the skillet and sauté for another 5 minutes, until the onion is golden and the poblanos are slightly charred and softened. Add the lime juice right at the end and toss to coat. Remove from the skillet.

MAKE THE LIME AIOLI: In a small bowl, mix together all of the ingredients until smooth. Taste: it should not need any salt; it should be tangy and zesty.

ASSEMBLE: Slice the rolls in half lengthwise. Spread a heaping tablespoon of aioli on the bottom half of each. On the top half, layer on the veggies evenly, then 2 to 3 romaine lettuce leaves, 2 slices of tomato, and 2 slices of cheese. Close the sandwiches.

LET'S GET TOASTY: Heat the same nonstick skillet over medium-high heat. Once the skillet is hot, add the sandwiches (one at a time), and place a cast-iron/heavy pan directly on top of the sandwich to press it down. This will provide the torta effect. Keep pressed for 2 to 3 minutes, until the bottom is golden. Using a spatula and your hands, carefully flip to the other side, and place the cast-iron pan on top again. Sear until the cheese is melted and the top of the sandwich is golden, about 2 minutes. Remove and let cool for 1 minute before cutting and serving. Enjoy immediately, or pack into your tiffin and enjoy at room temperature!

✕ ────────────────────────────

NOTE: You can substitute dried cayenne peppers for pequin chili peppers.

EIGHT

The SPANISH

TIFFIN

For whatever reason, I have been to Spain, or España, more times than I ever thought I would go during my short life. I'm not complaining, I just think it's quite random for me, since a lot of my travel destinations are based on food, history, and adventure. And if you know anything about the food in Spain, it's fairly limited for vegetarians, mainly because their culture is heavy on meat and seafood. But the food I did eat there was very good—supreme quality, simple, and with tons of olive oil. Some random observations I had about the Spaniards: they ate very late (I'm talking 10 p.m. dinners), they smoked a lot of cigarettes, and they loved their olive oil (and it was very, very good olive oil).

I was pleasantly surprised with the food, and having traveled there a few times in my life, I can say that Barcelona is one of my favorite European cities. It's beautiful, coastal (I love coastal cities), has tons of fabulous architecture and museums (thank you, Gaudí), has a rich history, and is very lively, and the people are welcoming. And yes, if you're wondering if La Sagrada Familia is still under construction, yes, yes, it is. Needless to say (because the chapter title is fairly self-explanatory), this chapter is dedicated to some of my favorite Spanish dishes, but with a slight Indian twist. And, of course, all with a little more spice!

One recipe that is not in this chapter but I absolutely loved stuffing in my face, morning and evening in Madrid, is *churros con chocolat*. I am still perfecting that recipe. Perhaps next book?

Baella

⇥ SERVES 2 ⇤

I happen to love my name for this dish, so I hope you're clapping for me. It's paella meets biryani, hence Baella! Don't tell me you don't find that clever. I ate a ton of paella throughout my travels in Spain—so much that I became sick of it. Not because it wasn't good, but I couldn't eat two servings of paella a day, every day! I would've turned into a rice ball! But I won't forget the richness and taste of a paella—the fresh vegetables, tomato base, saffron—and although the cooking style differs from a traditional Indian biryani, something about it reminded me of one.

What is a biryani, you ask? Biryani is a layered basmati rice dish that is cooked for hours in rich spices like cumin, coriander, saffron, cinnamon, and cloves. Some early recorded instances of biryani date back to the Mughal Empire in Northern India (present-day Delhi) and also in Hyderabad (South India). Biryanis are packed with flavor and can sometimes have a crispy bottom—similar to a paella. I wanted to emulate the concept of a paella but with biryani flavors, hence the Baella was born. If you cannot find Spanish bomba rice, then any short-grain rice will work.

1 tablespoon olive oil

½ teaspoon coriander seeds

½ teaspoon cumin seeds

1 (½-inch) piece fresh ginger, peeled and minced

1 clove garlic, minced

1 small white onion, diced

1 serrano chili pepper, minced

Pinch of kosher salt, plus more for seasoning

Pinch of freshly ground black pepper

1 roma tomato, diced

Heaping ¼ teaspoon sweet Spanish paprika

½ cup uncooked Spanish bomba (short-grain) rice—do not prewash, we need the starch!

Pinch of saffron threads

1 bay leaf

1 to 2 whole green cardamom pods

¼ cup frozen green peas

½ fresh lemon

GARNISHES

1 small white onion, thinly sliced

¼ cup unsweetened plain nondairy milk

1 tablespoon all-purpose flour

Olive oil

Kosher salt

2 tablespoons unsalted raw cashews

1 teaspoon vegan butter

2 tablespoons coarsely chopped fresh cilantro (stems and all!)

PREPARE THE RICE: In a large skillet, add the
1 tablespoon oil and place over medium-high heat.
While the skillet is heating up, coarsely grind the
coriander seeds and cumin seeds in a mortar and
pestle. Once the oil in the skillet is hot, add the
ground spices and toss to coat in the oil for about
30 seconds. Add the ginger, garlic, diced onion,
and serrano. Sauté for 2 to 3 minutes, until the onion
becomes translucent and sweats. Reduce the heat to
medium-low. Add the salt, black pepper, tomato, and
paprika. After about 2 minutes, the tomatoes should
begin to break down and become juicy.

NOW IT'S TIME TO ADD THE SPANISH bomba
rice; and toss to toast with the spice mixture. Once
the mixture is chunky, add about ¼ cup warm water,
the saffron threads, bay leaf, and cardamom pods
and mix. The mixture should be thick and fragrant.
Adjust the heat if you find that the rice mixture is
getting stuck to the skillet and it's drying too quickly.
Continue adding water, ¼ cup at a time, and mixing,
until you've added 2 cups (or a little more), ensuring
that the rice is immersed. Give the water portion a
quick taste and add more salt if necessary. Stir in
the frozen peas and cook, uncovered, for 12 to
15 minutes, until the water is absorbed and the rice
is cooked. (If the rice is not cooked and you find
the water has absorbed, just add more water and
continue cooking.) Remove from the heat, squeeze
½ fresh lemon wedge over the rice, and cover until
ready to serve.

MEANWHILE, PREPARE THE GARNISHES:
Place the sliced onion into a bowl with the nondairy
milk and mix to make sure all the onion slices are
separated and submerged. Place the flour in a zippy
bag. Set a medium skillet over medium-high heat
and add about 1 inch of oil. Once the oil has ripples
and is shimmering, it's hot! Using tongs, place the
onion in the zippy bag and give it a vigorous shake.
Once thoroughly coated, use the tongs to gently place
the onion into the hot oil, ensuring not to crowd the
skillet. Adjust the heat to medium, as we don't want
to burn the onion. Keep giving the onion a flip until
it's golden brown. Remove, drain on a paper towel–
lined plate, and immediately sprinkle with kosher
salt. Repeat until all the onion is cooked. Separately,
in a small skillet, toast the cashews with the vegan
butter over medium heat until golden.

SERVE: Uncover the Baella and sprinkle with
the cilantro, toasted cashews, and crispy onion.
If traveling, pack the Baella and the garnishes
into your tiffin separately. Top with the garnishes
before eating; enjoy!

Masala Marcona Almonds

⇥ MAKES 1 CUP ⇤

Smooth and buttery Marcona almonds meet the crackle and pop of curry leaves and red chili.

We all know regular almonds—you know, the ones grown in California that have a golden-brown skin and pointy oval shape? Yeah, those are good. But have you ever indulged yourself in a Marcona almond? Because these are the queen of almonds in my opinion! They're a little rounder than a traditional almond as we know it, skinless, smooth like butter, silky, and a product of Spain. I saw these everywhere while traveling through Spain and loved them. And I thought to myself, wouldn't these go great with some spicy Indian-esque masalas? Well, guess what, they do! I think the butteriness of the Marcona almond balances the heat of Indian spices really well.

My Masala Marcona Almonds are meant to be eaten as a snack, so you can make a whole batch and keep them in the pantry. You can even leave them out in a bowl in your kitchen or on your dining table, but I doubt they'll last that long!

MIX IT UP: In a medium bowl, mix together 1 teaspoon of the oil, the red chili powder, oregano, salt, and black pepper. Add the Marcona almonds and toss to coat thoroughly.

TOAST IT UP: Heat a medium skillet over medium-high heat and add the remaining 1 teaspoon oil. Once the oil is hot, add the cumin seeds and cook until they pop and become fragrant, about 30 seconds. Add the curry leaves, if using, and stand back, as these will pop aggressively. Once the popping subsides, swirl around in the oil and reduce the heat to medium-low. Add the seasoned Marcona almonds and toss in the skillet to spread evenly. Continue moving around and tossing in the skillet for 5 to 8 minutes (time varies based on intensity of flame and whether using an electric or gas stove), until the almonds become golden and the spices are aromatic.

COOL DOWN: Remove from the stove and spread out on a plate. Sprinkle with a pinch of fleur de sel, if using. Cool completely before serving. This lasts up to 2 weeks in an airtight container (if you can make it last that long!).

2 teaspoons good-quality olive oil

¼ teaspoon Kashmiri red chili powder

½ teaspoon dried oregano

⅛ teaspoon kosher salt

Pinch of freshly ground black pepper

1 heaping cup unsalted raw Marcona almonds

⅛ teaspoon cumin seeds

3 to 4 curry leaves (optional)

Pinch of fleur de sel (optional)

Cilantro-Olive Tapenade

⇥⟫ SERVES 2 ⟪⇤

As my friends and I were walking to our hotel in Barcelona, we were waiting at a traffic light on a sunny day and I looked to my left to see a beautiful bushy tree. I walked closer to it to discover that it was a green olive tree! On a busy street! I was born and raised in New York City, and we sure as hell didn't see any fruit or vegetable trees on random streets. And I just loved that this street was lined with olive trees. Naturally I picked one in an attempt to eat it, but it was not ready. Hey! I didn't say I was an expert in olive farming!

This story brings me to my Cilantro-Olive Tapenade. Olives are delicious in Spain and are incorporated so beautifully throughout the cuisine—whether it be a garnish on top of a tapa or sautéed into a dish or served as a dip, all of it is delicious. My Cilantro-Olive Tapenade is an ode to the delicious Manzanilla Spanish olives and my love for fresh cilantro. Trust me, it's a salty and herby match made in heaven! This is great on its own paired with some toast or crackers or even in a sandwich (almost muffuletta style).

- 1 cup Manzanilla olives, pitted
- 6 sprigs fresh cilantro (stems and all!)
- 1 red jalapeño or Fresno chili pepper, with a few slices reserved for garnish
- ½ teaspoon red pepper flakes
- ¼ teaspoon cumin powder
- 1 clove garlic
- Juice from ½ lemon
- 2 tablespoons extra-virgin olive oil, plus more for drizzling
- Crusty bread, for serving

PLACE ALL OF THE INGREDIENTS except the bread in a food processor and pulse until broken up and just combined—don't over-pulse as we don't want a mush, but rather a textured tapenade. Place into a shallow serving dish, drizzle with some more oil and some sliced red chili, if desired, and serve with crusty bread. This stays fresh for up to 1 week in an airtight container in the refrigerator. And I prefer it served at room temperature, so it's perfect for your tiffin.

Pan con Spicy Tomate

⇝ SERVES 2 ⇜

Aside from churros, *pan con tomate* was my absolute favorite dish in Spain: a thin baguette, typically Coca Bread, toasted to perfection and brushed with garlic, crushed tomato, tons of olive oil, and flaky sea salt. Again, there's a theme here with me—simple, street-food dishes really get me going! Somehow, I never got sick of eating *pan con tomate*. Perhaps because I'm a self-proclaimed "breaditarian" and will eat anything involving bread (good, warm, toasted bread specifically). Or maybe because I love tomatoes. We will never know. But what we do know is I have a delicious Pan con Spicy Tomate recipe for you that kicks it up a notch with the addition of serrano chili pepper and cumin. It's just a subtle hint—not too in-your-face—of spice. This is the perfect dish for traveling, too—just pack the bread in a separate section of the tiffin from the crushed tomato mixture, and dip at destination!

1 medium to large ripe beefsteak tomato

1 serrano chili pepper

2 cloves garlic

⅛ teaspoon cumin powder

Pinch of kosher salt

1 tablespoon good-quality olive oil, plus more for drizzling

½ loaf crusty Italian or French bread

Pinch of dried oregano, for garnish

Flaky sea salt, for garnish

LET'S GET JUICY: Place a box grater over a mixing bowl. Begin grating the tomato against the standard grate size. Be careful, as the tomato can be slippery. Grate until you get all the way down to the outer skin, and if that part gives you trouble grating, simply chop it up fine on a cutting board and add it to the bowl. The tomato should essentially become mush. Using the fine side of the box grater or a Microplane grater, grate the serrano and 1 garlic clove into the bowl of tomato. Add the cumin powder, salt, and 1 tablespoon of the oil and mix until combined. Set aside so all the flavors can come together.

TOAST THE BREAD: Place a medium nonstick skillet over medium heat. Slice the loaf in half lengthwise. Place the bread onto the skillet and toast for 3 to 4 minutes, until crispy and golden brown on the inside. While the bread is toasting, slice the remaining garlic clove in half lengthwise. Remove the bread from the skillet and place on the cutting board. Immediately rub the hot side of the bread with the garlic halves.

TOP AND SERVE: Top the bread with a generous helping of the spicy tomato mixture. Then drizzle with a little bit of oil, and top with a pinch each of oregano and flaky sea salt. If traveling, just pack the toast separately from the tomato mixture and you're good to go!

Patatas Karras

⇾ SERVES 2 ⇽

We've arrived at the final dish of my Spanish Tiffin chapter. I think I've expressed my love for potatoes earlier in the book. To me they are a bland porous vessel, which makes them great flavor picker-uppers! The traditional *patatas bravas* dish is slightly crisp golden-brown, cubed russet potatoes, generously drizzled with a garlic aioli and *brava* sauce (which is usually tomato- and paprika-based). You can't go wrong with potato, garlic, and spices. But it was always a tad bit bland for me—I tend to eat very spicy foods and the Spaniards do not. That didn't stop me from stuffing my face with *patatas bravas* in Spain, but it gave me the idea of spicing the dish up a bit.

My Patatas Karras—*karra* meaning "spicy" in Kannada—is the traditional Spanish *patatas bravas* but with a spicy tomato chutney and garlic aioli. See what I did there with the wordplay? I love the combination of starchy potatoes, creamy garlic, and spicy tomato chutney. It's like the love triangle that was always meant to be!

1 tablespoon olive oil

2 russet potatoes, peeled and cut into 1-inch chunks

GARLIC AIOLI

¼ cup nondairy mayonnaise

1 tablespoon nondairy sour cream

2 cloves garlic, coarsely chopped

Juice from ¼ lemon

Pinch of kosher salt, plus more for seasoning

Pinch of freshly ground black pepper

SPICY TOMATO CHUTNEY

1 teaspoon olive oil

⅛ teaspoon cumin seeds

1 dried red or cayenne chili

¼ cup tomato paste

½ teaspoon sweet Spanish paprika

½ teaspoon light agave, plus more for seasoning

Pinch of kosher salt, plus more for seasoning

Pinch of freshly ground black pepper

CRISP THE POTATOES: Place a large skillet over medium-high heat and pour in the 1 tablespoon oil. Once the oil is hot, add the potato—it should sizzle—and cook for about 1 minute. Lower the heat to medium-low and cook for 5 minutes, turning occasionally so all the sides get a chance to hit the hot oil. Once the potatoes start to get tender, increase the heat. We want to ensure that all sides achieve a golden-brown color and are slightly crisp. If you find that the skillet is getting dry, add more oil (I didn't say this was the healthiest dish!). After another 5 minutes, the potatoes should be crisp and pricked easily with a fork or toothpick. Transfer to a paper towel–lined plate to cool and drain any excess oil.

MAKE THE GARLIC AIOLI: Place all of the ingredients in a blender or use an immersion blender and blend everything until smooth, with no visible or large chunks of garlic. Taste and adjust for salt if necessary.

MAKE THE SPICY TOMATO CHUTNEY: Heat the 1 teaspoon oil in a small pan over medium heat. Once the oil is hot, add the cumin seeds and break up the dried red chili in the pan. After 30 seconds, the spices should be fragrant. Stir in the tomato paste. Once the tomato paste begins to thicken, after 30 to 60 seconds, add 3 tablespoons warm water. Lower the heat to medium-low and stir to create a thick sauce. Add the paprika, agave, salt, and black pepper. Keep stirring until the sauce begins to thicken. If it is too paste-like in consistency, add up to another tablespoon of warm water. Simmer for 2 to 3 minutes longer, until all the flavors mesh together. Then carefully remove, add to a small blender, and blend until super smooth. Pour back into the pan and taste to see if it needs more salt or agave (it can be too tart from the tomato paste). Transfer to a small bowl.

PLATE IT UP: Place the crisp potatoes on a serving dish and drizzle with both sauces generously. Serve immediately. If traveling, pack the sauces separate from the crisped potatoes, and plate at destination, or dip the potatoes into the sauces like fries!

NINE

The AUSTRALIAN

TIFFIN

T his is a special chapter for me. Why? Australia has been high on my bucket list of countries to visit, and I got the opportunity to crash my eldest sister's business trip and make it happen. Technically, she didn't invite me. I literally asked her at the dinner table one night and she couldn't resist my self-invite. I mean, who could resist me accompanying them on a trip?! But we had a good plan: I would stay with her in her hotel and one of her friends (or should I say mates) would accompany us so I had a buddy to explore the country with. And let me tell you, I saw a lot in ten days.

The other reason why this chapter is special to me is because Australia unexpectedly emerged as my top foodie country. You're probably wondering what I'm talking about, because when you hear Australia, you may think kangaroo burgers. Wrong! It is totally the opposite. Here is why I consider Australia to be at the pinnacle of food and cooking:

ALMOST EVERY INGREDIENT USED IN AUSTRALIA IS MADE IN AUSTRALIA, most being indigenous to Australia. This means the quality and taste of the individual ingredients is so much better than what I'm used to in the States.

AUSTRALIA'S PROXIMITY TO SOUTH ASIA AND ASIA PACIFIC means that there is an abundance of diversity in cuisines available; I had some of the best Indonesian, Malaysian, Indian, and Thai food in my life there.

BECAUSE AUSTRALIANS HAVE A TREMENDOUS AMOUNT OF RESPECT FOR THEIR ENVIRONMENT, there is a huge focus on plant-based food and sustainable farming. This meant that every restaurant I walked into had several (if not entire menus devoted to) plant-based items. My heart was singing. I have yet to see that in New York City.

For all these reasons and more, Australia is at the top of the food game. Not to mention, every dish I ate or drank there—from a simple Negroni on Bondi Beach to a delicious Vietnamese sweet corn treat in Melbourne—was delicious! This chapter focuses on recipes inspired by my travels through Australia, so if you can't get Down Under soon, hopefully these recipes will transport you there!

Avocado & Spicy Peanut Chutney Toast

⇥ SERVES 2 ⇤

Did you know avo toast is from Down Under? Yup! It was created in the 1990s in Sydney by chef Bill Granger. And some of the natives at Bondi Beach claim it happened in their area of Sydney. I actually learned this all on Day 1 during my first meal in Sydney, which was at a small café situated right on Bondi Beach. So naturally I ordered an avocado toast. Let me preface this by saying that I am not one of those "basic" brunch–goers who orders an avocado toast everywhere they go (I tend to find it bland and unfulfilling). But I was at the birthplace of avocado toast, so I had to indulge!

As I mentioned in the introduction to this chapter, all of the ingredients in Australia are grown in Australia, so right off the bat the avocado has such a rich and buttery flavor. My Avocado & Spicy Peanut Chutney Toast brings together the sunny, fresh flavors of an Aussie avocado toast with a kick of a traditional dry chutney we eat at home, called a peanut chutney. I love this combination and hope you do, too. It's an unlikely but devilishly good combination!

DRY PEANUT CHUTNEY

- ½ cup unsalted dry-roasted peanuts
- 2 dried red chilies
- ½ teaspoon cumin seeds
- Pinch of kosher salt
- Pinch of freshly ground black pepper

- 4 slices thick crusty bread, such as sourdough, Italian loaf, or ciabatta
- 2 tablespoons vegan butter, at room temperature
- 2 Hass avocados, slit in half, seed removed, and thinly sliced
- ½ fresh lemon
- 2 tablespoons pomegranate kernels
- 2 tablespoons chopped fresh cilantro leaves
- 1 tablespoon olive oil
- Pinch of kosher salt

Method follows

MAKE THE DRY PEANUT CHUTNEY: In a food processor, add the peanuts, dried chilies, cumin seeds, salt, and black pepper. Pulse until the mixture is just combined—it should be coarsely chopped and slightly chunky. Taste—it should be spicy, salty, and slightly smoky. Place in a jar and set aside.

MAKE THE AVOCADO TOAST: Place a small nonstick skillet over medium heat. Butter up each side of the 4 slices of bread. Once the skillet is hot, add the slices, one at a time, and toast for 2 to 3 minutes on each side until golden brown. While the bread is toasting, get the remaining ingredients prepped and ready—the avocados, lemon, pomegranate kernels, cilantro leaves, oil, and salt. Transfer the toasts to a serving platter.

ASSEMBLY TIME: Layer the avocado onto each slice. Drizzle ½ teaspoon of the oil onto each toast. Squeeze the juice from the lemon onto the avocado across all the toasts and sprinkle with a pinch of salt. Top each slice with a heaping tablespoon of peanut chutney, cilantro, and pomegranate seeds. This toast is great eaten immediately or packed and eaten at a later time. A tip if packing: hold the salt. Salt lets out a lot of moisture from the avocado, so leaving the salt out will allow the avocado to retain its texture. And if you use thick and crusty bread, it will retain its texture even with the avocado on top. Plus, the spicy peanut chutney and pomegranate hold well, so when you eat this later, it won't be all mush—it'll be perfect!

Watermelon Rose Salad

 **SERVES 2**

Obviously, I did a ton of research before traveling to Australia—mainly food research (the only kind of research there is, duh). And Black Star Pastry kept popping up. Why? Because apparently, they had one the most internet-famous cakes in the world: Strawberry Watermelon Cake. I am certainly not one of those individuals who believes everything they read on the internet, so I decided to do some hands-on research, also known as physically going to the bakery (which happened to be conveniently located right by our hotel) to get a slice of this famous cake.

I love both strawberry and watermelon, so I am the core audience for this kind of cake, but I still did not know what to expect. First, it was beautiful to look at, and I am a visual eater first and foremost. Second, it has a lovely texture when dug into with a spoon—slightly crisp, creamy, and juicy. Third, it was delicious. Light and airy, yet sweet and floral. I loved it and ate the whole thing. I knew that once I left Australia, I probably wouldn't encounter this exact cake again, so my Watermelon Rose Salad emulates some of the same flavors of the cake but in a savory salad form! Trust me, the rose pairs so well with the watermelon and the spice of the Fresno chili pepper. The key is to use the rose essence sparingly, as a little goes a long way. This salad is a visual pleaser and is also perfect for outdoor lunches or picnics, if you're into that sort of thing.

1 red Fresno chili pepper, minced

1 scallion, thinly sliced, white and green parts separated

½ teaspoon rose essence or rose water

½ teaspoon dried thyme

½ fresh lemon

Pinch of kosher salt

Pinch of freshly ground black pepper

3 to 4 tablespoons olive oil

2 cups fresh watermelon, cubed

¼ cup fresh mint leaves

TAHINI LEMON CREMA

½ cup nondairy sour cream

¼ cup tahini paste

1 teaspoon fresh lemon zest

Juice from ½ lemon

Pinch of kosher salt

Pinch of freshly ground black pepper

Method follows

PREPARE THE DRESSING: In a large bowl, combine the Fresno pepper, white parts of the scallion, rose essence, thyme, lemon juice, salt, and black pepper. While mixing, drizzle in the oil until well combined and emulsified. Taste to check for salt and add more if necessary. Add the watermelon cubes and toss to coat thoroughly. Set aside and let the dressing seep in for 10 minutes.

MAKE THE CREMA: Place the sour cream, tahini paste, lemon zest, lemon juice, salt, and pepper in a food processor or blender. Blend until very smooth with no visible lumps. If the mixture is very thick and grainy, add 1 to 3 tablespoons water and blend until it becomes a creamy paste, similar to the consistency of a smooth cream cheese.

PLATE IT UP: On a large serving dish, spread the crema in a thick layer. Then top with the watermelon salad. Garnish with the mint leaves and green parts of the scallion. Serve immediately. If traveling, pack the dressed watermelon salad separate from the crema. And the longer the watermelon marinates in the dressing, the yummier it tastes!

Baby Eggplants in Peanut-Basil Sauce

 SERVES 2

This is one of the more unique dishes in the book. It a combination of Indian and Vietnamese flavors, which I think is so overlooked as a combination of cuisines. There are so many similarities between Indian and Vietnamese cuisine—the spices, variance in textures, balance of flavors—it's the best mashup!

While at a restaurant called Chin Chin in Sydney, I ordered their stuffed baby eggplant dish. I have a certain idea of what a stuffed baby eggplant dish should look and taste like, because it is a staple in our household and in Maharashtrian/Karnatakan cooking. It's generally seared baby eggplants, stuffed with a spicy onion, ginger, and garlic mixture and simmered in a spicy peanut-based gravy with black mustard seeds, curry leaves, chilies, and fresh cilantro. The stuffed eggplant dish at Chin Chin was almost identical with the exception of the curry leaves and black mustard seeds, using instead kaffir lime leaves, Thai basil, and coconut cream. It was velvety, spicy, and reminded me of the eggplant we made at home but with a slightly different taste. My Baby Eggplants in Peanut-Basil Sauce is a true combination of the traditional Indian stuffed baby eggplants we make at home with this slightly Vietnamese-Thai stuffed eggplant dish from Chin Chin. It is the perfect dish to make on a cold winter night and paired with some steamed jasmine or basmati rice—it's a winner!

6 baby eggplants

2 tablespoons neutral oil

¼ teaspoon fennel seeds

¼ teaspoon coriander seeds

1 medium yellow onion, diced

2 serrano chili peppers, minced

2 cloves garlic, minced

1 (1-inch) piece fresh ginger, peeled and minced

½ teaspoon turmeric powder

¼ teaspoon kosher salt

Pinch of freshly ground black pepper

¼ cup ground unsalted dry-roasted peanuts

2 to 4 tablespoons water

PEANUT-BASIL SAUCE

1 tablespoon neutral oil, plus more for shallow frying

¼ teaspoon fennel seeds

¼ teaspoon coriander seeds

½ cup smooth unsalted natural peanut butter

½ teaspoon turmeric powder

¼ teaspoon red chili powder

1 teaspoon jaggery or light agave

Kosher salt and freshly ground black pepper

Juice from ¼ lemon

3 sprigs fresh Thai basil, leaves picked off and coarsely chopped, plus 2 sprigs

2 tablespoons unsweetened coconut cream, for garnish

FILL THE EGGPLANTS: Place a large nonstick skillet over medium-high heat and pour in 2 teaspoons of the neutral oil. While the oil heats, coarsely grind the fennel seeds and coriander seeds in a mortar and pestle. Add the ground spices to the hot oil and sauté for about 30 seconds, until fragrant and the spices start popping in the oil. Add the onion, serrano, garlic, and ginger. Sauté for 2 to

3 minutes, until the onion starts becoming translucent. Add the turmeric, salt, and black pepper. Cook for 3 to 4 minutes, until the onion is soft, but not browned. Add the ground peanuts and mix until well combined. Add water in 1-tablespoon increments—the mixture should be thick and almost like a paste, not runny. Adjust your water accordingly. Cook for another 2 to 4 minutes, until very soft. Taste and add more salt if necessary. Transfer to a bowl to cool to room temperature. Meanwhile, using a sharp paring knife, make four slits at the butt of each eggplant to create a slight opening. Gently stuff each eggplant with the filling, making sure to get as much as possible in there without breaking the eggplants. Continue until all the eggplants are stuffed. You should have about half the filling left over.

SAUTÉ THE EGGPLANTS: Using the same skillet, after wiping with a moistened towel, place it over high heat and add the remaining 1 teaspoon neutral oil. Once the oil is hot, add the stuffed eggplants and sear on each side for 5 to 7 minutes, until darkened and blistered. They should be soft enough for a paring knife to easily go through, but you don't want the eggplants to be mushy. Transfer to a plate and set aside.

SAUCE TIME: Using the same skillet, pour in the neutral oil and, once hot, add the fennel seeds and coriander seeds. Sauté for 30 seconds. Add the reserved eggplant stuffing and sauté for about 2 minutes, then add the peanut butter, turmeric, and chili powder. Mix well and, after about another minute, add ½ cup water. Stir in the jaggery and a

pinch of salt and black pepper. Reduce the heat to low and simmer, continuing to add up to another ½ cup water, as the mixture will thicken up and we want to maintain a thick sauce consistency. Either using an immersion blender or transferring to a regular blender, blend half of the mixture until super smooth and pour it back into the sauce. The consistency should be smooth with some texture. Taste for salt and add the lemon juice. Once thick and cooked through, add the chopped Thai basil and the stuffed eggplants. Cover with a lid and let the eggplants cook through with the steam for 8 to 10 minutes. The eggplants should be fork-tender. Turn off the heat and keep covered until ready to serve.

CRISP THE BASIL: In a small skillet, add a 1-inch-thick layer of neutral oil and place over medium-high heat. Once the oil has ripples and is shimmering, it's hot! Pick off the Thai basil leaves from the reserved 2 sprigs and carefully add them to the hot oil. Lower the heat to medium and fry the basil for 30 seconds or so on each side, until darkened and crisp. Transfer to a paper towel–lined plate to drain the excess oil. Immediately sprinkle with a pinch of salt.

GARNISH: Drizzle the coconut cream on top of the stuffed eggplants, top with the crispy Thai basil, and serve over rice or with naan or roti! If traveling, pack your stuffed eggplants in one tiffin compartment, while packing your roti/rice in another compartment.

Chocolate Cardamom Macadamia Butter

⇒ MAKES ABOUT 1 CUP ⇐

I noticed all sorts of delicious things in Australia, but one thing I noticed in particular was macadamias—macadamia milk, whole macadamias, macadamias on menus—they popped up everywhere! And I learned that Australia is the world's largest producer of macadamia nuts, because they are *only* indigenous to Australia. No, not Hawaii, even though I was convinced that they were after a trip to a macadamia nut plantation on Maui when I was ten. It turns out, there were a lot of native Australian plants, foods, and animals that were taken to Hawaii and cultivated there. For instance, the forests we see in the classic *Jurassic Park* movies are all shot in Hawaii, but what people don't know is that the Jurassic-era plantation only exists in present-day Australia. So, they replicated some of that vegetation in Hawaii for the movie! Interesting, right?

Anyway, back to macadamia nuts. They were so good in Australia—super creamy, buttery, and wholesome. I wanted to bring some of that feel to our homes with my Chocolate Cardamom Macadamia Butter, which can be spread on toast, pancakes, over fruit—really anything! Make it as smooth or chunky as you like. There aren't too many rules here.

1 cup unsalted raw macadamia nuts

3 heaping tablespoons unsweetened good-quality cocoa powder

1 teaspoon coconut oil

3 to 4 tablespoons light agave

½ teaspoon freshly ground cardamom

Pinch of kosher salt

IN A FOOD PROCESSOR, pulse the macadamia nuts until they start breaking down and becoming smooth. Add the cocoa powder, oil, and 3 tablespoons agave and continue blending until the mixture gets super smooth. Add the ground cardamom and salt. Give it a taste and add up to another tablespoon agave if you prefer a sweeter spread. This can be stored in a jar or airtight container in a cool and dry place for several weeks.

Bondi Blue Tea Cakes

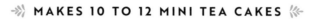

MAKES 10 TO 12 MINI TEA CAKES

Australia is beautiful—there is absolutely no doubt about it. The terrain is varied from city to city and along the coast. You can have the misty Blue Mountains just north of Sydney, penguins on the coast of Melbourne, and the white sand beaches on the outskirts of downtown Sydney. But something that is unforgettable is the blue hue of the ocean, specifically at Bondi Beach. It's one of the best known and most popular beaches in Australia, and there's a reason for it. The minute you get a peek at the ocean when approaching by taxi, you're blown away by the turquoise blue. It almost looks fake! Then you step atop Icebergs, a touristy landmark, to get a stunning view of the famous pools parallel to the wavy beach. It was my first stop in Australia and one of my favorites. (I, of course, had a 30-minute photo shoot of me sipping a Negroni right by the beach, but I digress.)

My Bondi Blue Tea Cakes embody the freshness and beautiful blue hue of Bondi Beach via a plant—butterfly pea flowers! These beautiful Southeast Asian flowers have minimal to no flavor but a stunning blue color that easily bleeds into any warm liquid. They are perfect for creating that perfect blue drizzle for our tea cakes. Eat these tea cakes by a beach (or just pretend that you're by one) and enjoy!

TEA CAKES

Baking spray

4 tablespoons vegan butter, at room temperature

¾ cup raw cane sugar

3 tablespoons vegan egg substitute

1 teaspoon vanilla extract

2½ cups all-purpose flour

1 teaspoon baking powder

⅛ teaspoon baking soda

¼ teaspoon kosher salt

½ cup plus 2 tablespoons vegan cream cheese or sour cream, at room temperature

¼ cup unsweetened nondairy milk

1 teaspoon fresh orange zest

BONDI BLUE GLAZE

1 heaping tablespoon dried butterfly pea flowers

¼ cup water

1 cup powdered sugar, sifted

1 tablespoon unsweetened nondairy milk

Blue cornflowers, for garnish (optional)

Method follows

PREHEAT THE OVEN TO 350°F. Spray a mini Bundt cupcake or tea cake pan until thoroughly coated. Set aside.

MAKE THE CAKE: In a stand mixer with the paddle attachment, whip together the butter and sugar until light in color and fluffy. Switch to low speed and pour in the egg substitute; mix until combined. Add the vanilla extract to combine. Turn off the mixer and scrape the bowl down. In a separate bowl, combine the flour, baking powder, baking soda, and salt. Turn the mixer on low, add half the flour mixture, and mix. Then add half of the sour cream and mix. Add the remaining flour mixture, then the remaining sour cream. Mix until no streaks appear. Mix in the nondairy milk until just combined. Scrape down with a spatula. Remove from the stand mixer and stir in the orange zest. The batter will be thick!

POUR AND BAKE: Pour into the prepared mini Bundt cake pan and bake for 25 to 30 minutes, or until a toothpick inserted in the center comes out clean. Remove and let cool completely.

MAKE THE BONDI BLUE GLAZE: In a small pot, add the butterfly pea flowers with ¼ cup water and bring to a simmer. The natural blue dye from the flowers should bleed into the water. Simmer for 2 to 3 minutes, until the flowers have been completely drained of their colors. Strain into a bowl to remove the flowers. Discard the flowers and let the water cool to room temperature. In a separate bowl, mix together the powdered sugar and nondairy milk until smooth. Add 1 tablespoon of the blue water and mix until bright blue. Keep mixing and adding the blue water 1 tablespoon at a time until the glaze is bright blue—like the ocean—and slightly thinner than a sugar cookie glaze. Let cool completely.

GLAZE THE CAKES: Flip the cooled cakes out of the Bundt pan. Drizzle on the blue glaze until the tops are slightly covered. Top with blue cornflowers, if using, and set aside for at least 10 minutes before serving. These last up to 1 week in an airtight container so can easily travel in your tiffin.

TEN

The
MIDDLE EASTERN

❧❧❧❧❀❧❧❧❧

TIFFIN

I haven't traveled as much in the Middle East as I have wished. I think most Americans (and especially women) are cautious about traveling to the Middle East, given the reputation it has (and how that is presented to Americans), which I don't wholeheartedly agree with. But this is a cookbook, not a book on American politics and propaganda. That being said, I have tasted a ton of delicious Middle Eastern food through my travels in the States, India, and Dubai, comprising Turkish, Lebanese, Iranian, and Egyptian food mostly. And the consensus has always been—it is f****g delicious! Not to mention, there is so much variety for vegetarians and vegans. I love the freshness of the food—with the heavy use of lemon, fresh mint, pomegranate, and garlic—and I love the variation between sweet and spicy. It also reminds me a bit of Indian cuisine, because Middle Eastern desserts tend to be diabetically sweet, just like Indian desserts (I am only half joking).

So why am I writing a chapter on Middle Eastern food without having traveled to many of the countries? Well, a few reasons. One—I love it, and I want to include it so everyone can experience the deliciousness. Two—I have visited Dubai, lived in London for six months when I was in college, and traveled extensively through Greece (which has a lot of Middle Eastern influence), which all expanded my horizons on the variations of Middle Eastern food. And three—my parents visited Egypt some years ago, and by the transient property, it's like I visited, too! This chapter is a compilation of some of my favorite Middle Eastern dishes—some with a slight Indian twist, and all with a Chef Priyanka touch, of course!

Falafel-Pear Lettuce Wraps

 SERVES 2

Falafel is probably one of the best-known Middle Eastern dishes worldwide. Delicious legume-based fritters topped with creamy tahini, a salad, sometimes pickled veggies, hot sauce, and wrapped in a fresh pita. Drooling yet? And it's a street food, so, what d'ya know, Priyanka loves it! But what I don't think people know is that falafel varies from country to country and culture to culture. For instance, in Egypt, falafel is traditionally made with fava (or broad) beans and then is smashed into a large, hot thin pita and rolled up—this is how my parents described it was done on the streets of Cairo! And in Israel, falafel is usually made only with chickpeas and served whole in a thicker pita. And I'm sure there is a Lebanese version, a Palestinian version, and so on and so forth.

All you need to know is that this recipe is the Chef Priyanka version with a twist—a crispy baked falafel patty topped with a garlic tahini and . . . wait for it . . . seared cumin pears. This generally has no business being in falafels, but the sweetness, texture, and hint of cumin pair beautifully with the falafel. I serve these up in lettuce wraps (cause I'm healthy, duh), but you're welcome to eat this as a platter or inside your favorite pita!

FALAFEL PATTIES

- ¼ teaspoon cumin seeds
- ¼ teaspoon coriander seeds
- 7 ounces (about ½ standard can) low-sodium chickpeas, rinsed and drained
- 7 ounces (heaping ½ cup) frozen fava beans, thawed
- 1 small red onion, coarsely chopped
- 2 cloves garlic
- 2 Indian green chilies or 2 serrano chili peppers
- 5 to 6 full sprigs flat-leaf parsley, coarsely chopped
- 4 to 5 full sprigs fresh cilantro, coarsely chopped (stems and all!)
- ½ teaspoon baking soda
- Pinch of kosher salt
- Pinch of freshly ground black pepper
- ¼ cup stale bread, made into bread crumbs (or plain bread crumbs)
- Olive oil, for cooking

GARLIC TAHINI

- ¼ cup tahini paste, stirred
- ¼ cup unsweetened plain nondairy yogurt
- 1 clove garlic, coarsely chopped
- Juice from ¼ lemon
- Pinch of kosher salt
- 2 to 3 tablespoons warm water

CUMIN PEARS

- 1 teaspoon olive oil
- 1 Bosc pear, peel on, core removed, and sliced thin lengthwise
- ⅛ teaspoon cumin powder
- Kosher salt and freshly ground black pepper

- 6 leaves butter lettuce
- ¼ cup grape tomatoes, sliced in half lengthwise
- 1 scallion, thinly sliced on the bias

Method follows

MAKE THE FALAFEL PATTIES: In a large skillet, toast the cumin seeds and coriander seeds over medium-low heat for 2 minutes until fragrant. Transfer to a mortar and pestle and grind to a coarse texture. In a food processor, add the chickpeas, fava beans, onion, garlic, green chilies, ground spices, parsley, cilantro, baking soda, salt, and black pepper. Pulse 5 or 6 times, until the mixture is broken down and just combined. Don't overmix, as we're not trying to create a hummus! Once the texture of the dough looks like it's sticking together when pressed between two fingers, transfer to a mixing bowl, add the bread crumbs, and mix. Give it a taste—it should taste herby, spicy, and garlicky. Add more salt if necessary. Using a mini scooper, scoop one ball and roll and slightly press down to form a small patty. Repeat with the rest of the dough. Place the patties on a parchment-lined cookie sheet and set in the refrigerator for at least 15 minutes, until firm.

MAKE THE GARLIC TAHINI: While the falafel patties are chillin' in the fridge, make the tahini. Rinse out the food processor and place all of the ingredients, except the water, in it. Blend until smooth with no visible lumps or chunks of garlic. If the mixture is very thick like a paste, blend in a tablespoon at a time of warm water until you achieve a creamy texture. Set aside.

BAKE UP THE FALAFEL PATTIES: Preheat the oven to 375°F. Set the same large skillet used for the spices over medium-high heat. Pour in about 1 tablespoon of olive oil. Once the oil is hot, add the falafel patties and sear on each side for 3 to 5 minutes, using a set of tongs to flip carefully, until golden brown and firm but not hard to touch. Then transfer to the same parchment-lined cookie sheet. Bake for 10 to 12 minutes, until completely heated through, cooked on the sides, and very firm to the touch. Remove and cool for 2 minutes.

MAKE THE CUMIN PEARS: While the falafels bake and cool, prepare the pears. Wipe down the same large skillet, set over medium heat, and add the olive oil. Once hot, add the sliced pears and sauté in the olive oil for 1 to 2 minutes, until there is some caramelization on the edges of the pears. Sprinkle in the cumin powder, a pinch of salt, and 2 grinds of black pepper. Sauté for 2 to 3 minutes, until the pears have softened to fork-tender and are golden, but still intact. Remove and set aside.

ASSEMBLE: Place the butter lettuce leaves on a platter. Layer 1 to 2 falafel patties onto each leaf, top with 2 to 4 slices of pear, grape tomatoes, a drizzle of tahini, and a garnish of scallions. If traveling, chop the lettuce up and toss with the tomatoes and scallions and place in one container. Layer on the cumin pears, then the falafel patties, and pack the tahini separately to make for a falafel salad bowl.

Creamy Parsley Tahini Dressing

⇝ MAKES 1½ CUPS ⇜

I don't think there is too much to say about this recipe, aside from the fact that it's creamy, zesty, and you can literally pour it on everything (perhaps even bathe in it, if that's your thing). I love the simplicity and how the Middle Eastern flavors really come through. This dressing is great to use as an alternative with the falafels on page 171, on top of a salad, in a sandwich, or even just as a dip. Another clever use is tossing it with some boiled farfalle or penne to make for a Middle Eastern–inspired pasta salad! Plus, it keeps in the fridge for up to 2 weeks!

½ cup tahini paste

½ cup flat-leaf parsley

¼ teaspoon cumin powder

½ fresh lemon

Pinch of kosher salt

Pinch of freshly ground black pepper

1 tablespoon olive oil

¼ to ½ cup room-temperature water

PLACE ALL INGREDIENTS in the food processor or blender, with the exception of the warm water. Blend until smooth. The texture will be similar to a thick paste.

WHILE ON LOW SPEED, drizzle in the warm water, starting with ¼ cup. Continue blending until a thick, creamy dressing texture is achieved. If you prefer a thinner consistency, add up to another ¼ cup water. There should be no visible lumps and all the parsley should be blended into the dressing; the color will be a light earthy green.

POUR INTO A MASON JAR, airtight container, or my preferred vessel—a squeezy bottle with a cap. This makes it easy to drizzle onto anything! This dressing is best at room temperature, so it's perfect for traveling.

Sweet 'n' Tangy Brussels Sprouts

⇒⇒ SERVES 2 ⇐⇐

Brussels sprouts are underrated, but they can also be overrated. I feel as though I see the same (or similar) recipes for Brussels sprouts constantly in rotation online. Ehh, boring. I will admit, I didn't grow up eating Brussels sprouts—it's not a vegetable that is within Indian cuisine, so naturally it didn't make it to our dinner table often. I really began to appreciate Brussels sprouts in Middle Eastern dishes. There are so many Brussels sprout dishes on the menus at Lebanese and Turkish restaurants in New York City, and one of my favorite restaurants in particular, ilili, makes a Brussels sprout dish that is roasted and tossed with blistered grapes, almonds, and labneh. How delicious does that sound?

My Sweet 'n' Tangy Brussels Sprouts combines some of the elements I've enjoyed eating at my favorite Middle Eastern restaurants, and also some traditional Middle Eastern elements like pomegranate, dates, and almonds. All the good stuff! So, if you are *still* a Brussels sprouts hater from when you were younger, I recommend giving this dish a chance—you may sprout a new interest in it, ha!

ROASTED BRUSSELS SPROUTS

3 tablespoons olive oil

Heaping ½ teaspoon red pepper flakes

1 teaspoon dried thyme

¼ teaspoon cumin powder

¼ teaspoon coriander powder

Pinch of kosher salt

Pinch of freshly ground black pepper

¼ wedge fresh lemon

2 cups Brussels sprouts, sliced in half

POMEGRANATE GLAZE

½ cup pomegranate juice

2 tablespoons raw cane sugar

2 tablespoons slivered almonds, lightly toasted

6 dates, coarsely chopped

ALMOND YOGURT SAUCE

Heaping ¼ cup unsweetened plain almond yogurt

2 tablespoons tahini paste

1 dried red chili

⅛ teaspoon cumin seeds

Pinch of kosher salt

Pinch of freshly ground black pepper

1 to 2 teaspoons olive oil

FOR SERVING

2 to 3 tablespoons microgreens (optional)

1 scallion, thinly sliced on the bias

2 tablespoons coarsely chopped fresh mint

2 pitas, warmed (optional)

MARINATE AND ROAST: Preheat the oven to 375°F. Line a baking sheet with parchment paper. In a large bowl, add the oil, red chili flakes, thyme, cumin powder, coriander powder, salt, black pepper, and the lemon juice from the lemon wedge. Stir and taste. Add more salt if necessary. Add the Brussels sprouts and toss to coat thoroughly. Spread evenly on the prepared baking sheet and bake for 30 to 35 minutes, until fork-tender and charred.

MEANWHILE, MAKE THE POMEGRANATE GLAZE: Pour the pomegranate juice into a small pot and add the sugar. Place over medium-low heat and bring to a boil. Reduce the flame to low and let simmer, mixing occasionally, for 30 to 35 minutes, until the mixture reduces and becomes almost molasses-like in texture. Remove from the heat and cool to room temperature.

BRUSSELS MEET POMEGRANATE: Once the Brussels sprouts have cooled to room temperature, toss in a large bowl with the pomegranate glaze, until completely coated. Add the slivered toasted almonds and dates. Give it a taste. If it tastes too sweet, add a bit more salt. The flavors should be balanced between sweet, tangy, and spicy.

MAKE THE ALMOND YOGURT SAUCE: Place all of the ingredients into a blender and blend until super smooth with no visible lumps or chunks.

PLATE AND SERVE: Place a large dollop of the Almond Yogurt Sauce on the bottom of a shallow bowl or platter. Spread out evenly. Pile on the glazed Brussels sprouts and top with the microgreens, if using, scallions, and fresh mint. If eating immediately, serve with a warm pita, if you'd like, and dig in! If traveling, layer the Brussels sprouts directly into your tiffin. The microgreens in this case are optional, as they might wilt in travel.

Spinach-stuffed Eggplant Rolls with Mint-Walnut Crunch

 SERVES 2

Eggplant is a staple in many global cuisines; it is surely a staple in Indian cooking! And I learned that it's quite prominent in Greek and Middle Eastern cuisine, too. My favorite Lebanese and Egyptian restaurants in New York City always have some warm eggplant dishes (which I obviously always order).

One of the best eggplant dishes I ever had was when I traveled through Greece with my friends in college. On Mykonos, we rented ATVs to navigate the small and windy roads on the island. We stumbled upon the cutest Greek restaurant situated on a side street, painted white and covered with what looked similar to pink dogwood trees. I ordered one of the select vegetarian dishes on the menu—a whole roasted and stuffed eggplant. It was seared to perfection and so garlicky and delicious. And it tasted like it had a bit of Middle Eastern flair—a hint of flat-leaf parsley, cumin, and olive oil. I wanted to create a dish that brought together the flavors I tasted in Greece with some of my favorite eggplant dishes at my local Middle Eastern restaurant in New York City. Thus, these Spinach-stuffed Eggplant Rolls were born!

MINT-PARSLEY SAUCE

- 1 bunch fresh mint (about 2 cups of leaves)
- 2 bunches fresh flat-leaf parsley
- 1 dried red chili
- Pinch of kosher salt
- Pinch of freshly ground black pepper
- Juice from ¼ lemon
- 1 tablespoon good-quality olive oil

EGGPLANT AND FILLING

- 1 large Italian eggplant, cut into 8 to 10 (¼-inch) slices lengthwise
- ½ teaspoon cumin seeds
- ½ teaspoon coriander seeds
- ¼ teaspoon red chili powder
- Pinch of freshly grated nutmeg
- 1 tablespoon plus 1 teaspoon olive oil
- ½ white onion, finely chopped
- 2 cloves garlic, minced
- 2 cups baby spinach, chopped
- Kosher salt

- 1 scallion, thinly sliced on the bias, for garnish
- 2 tablespoons unsalted walnuts, lightly roasted and chopped, for garnish

Method follows

MAKE THE SAUCE: In a food processor or blender, pulse together the mint, parsley, red chili, salt, and black pepper. Transfer to a bowl. Squeeze in the lemon juice and stir in the 1 tablespoon oil. The texture should be similar to a chimichurri. Set aside so the flavors can blend together as you prepare the other ingredients.

PREPARE THE EGGPLANT: Place a rack on a large sheet pan and lay the eggplant slices on top. Salt each slice on both sides and let rest for 10 minutes. This helps the bitterness of the eggplant release. After 10 minutes, thoroughly rinse the eggplant and pat with a kitchen or paper towel until dry.

GRIND THE SPICES: While the eggplant rests, place the cumin seeds, coriander seeds, red chili powder, and nutmeg in a mortar and pestle and crush to a coarse grind.

LET'S GET COOKIN': Place a large nonstick skillet over medium-high heat. Add the 1 tablespoon oil. Once hot, add the eggplant slices, making sure not to crowd the pan. Cook on each side for 3 to 5 minutes, using tongs to flip, until tender and browned. Transfer to a paper towel–lined plate to drain excess oil.

MAKE THE FILLING: Wipe the skillet down with a paper towel. Add the 1 teaspoon oil over medium-low heat. Once hot, add the spices from the mortar and pestle and let sizzle for 30 seconds until fragrant. Then add the onion and garlic and sauté until the onion is slightly translucent, 3 to 4 minutes. Next, add the spinach. Sprinkle with a pinch of salt—just a pinch, as remember spinach wilts down to less than 50 percent of its size! Sauté until reduced in size and softened. Taste and add more salt if necessary. Remove from the heat and let cool to room temperature.

ROLL AND SERVE: Place about ½ to 1 tablespoon of filling on the end of 1 eggplant slice. Gently roll until closed and place on a serving dish. Repeat until all the eggplant slices are stuffed and rolled. Top with the Mint-Parsley Sauce and garnish with scallion and toasted walnuts. These travel really well, so don't be afraid to pack them up in your tiffin and hit the road!

Almond-Tahini Cake with Rose Syrup & Pistachio

SERVES 2 OR MAKES 1 MINI LOAF

Now, I know I'm not meant to have any favorites, because all of these recipes are my children, but if I had to choose one for this chapter it would be this dish. Aside from the fact that I have a ginormous sweet tooth (it's always so hard for me to pick between spicy and sweet because I like them both so much . . . but I generally gravitate toward the sweet), this cake tastes like baklava—but without all the effort of the delicate layering and buttering of a baklava. When I think about Middle Eastern desserts, there are a few core flavors that come to mind—orange blossom water, rose water, nuts, and something cakey or flakey. And I'm here to report that this delicate almond-tahini cake soaked with a sweet rose syrup and topped with buttery green pistachios delivers just that! It's almost like I'm being transported to the beautiful city of Istanbul or the deserts of Egypt . . . okay, I may be getting carried away, but I believe that food *should* transport you. I hope you bake this cake and it takes you on a Middle Eastern journey. Happy baking!

ALMOND TAHINI LOAF

Baking spray or vegan butter, for coating

1 cup plus 2 tablespoons all-purpose flour

1 teaspoon baking soda

½ teaspoon baking powder

¼ teaspoon salt

2 tablespoons plus 2 teaspoons tahini, stirred

2 tablespoons plus 2 teaspoons vegetable oil or coconut oil

1 cup unsweetened plain full-fat almond or coconut milk

½ cup raw cane sugar

½ teaspoon almond extract

ROSE GLAZE

½ cup raw cane sugar

1 teaspoon rose essence or rose water

¼ teaspoon fresh lemon or orange juice (optional, but helps prevent crystallization of glaze)

2 tablespoons dried rose petals, plus more for garnish

1 heaping tablespoon chopped unsalted pistachios

Method follows

PREP: Preheat the oven to 350°F. Spray or butter a standard 9 x 5-inch loaf pan.

BATTER UP: In a large bowl or the bowl of a stand mixer, sift together all of the dry ingredients and set aside. In a medium bowl, using a whisk, mix together the tahini, oil, and almond milk until well combined. Using a hand mixer or the stand mixer fitted with the paddle attachment on low speed, pour the wet ingredients into the dry ingredients. Mix until combined—but do not overbeat! Add the sugar and almond extract and mix until combined.

BAKE IT: Pour the batter into the prepared loaf pan (it will fill halfway up the pan to make half the size of a standard loaf) and bake for 30 to 35 minutes, until slightly golden brown and an inserted toothpick comes out clean.

MEANWHILE, MAKE THE ROSE GLAZE: In a small pot, combine the sugar with ½ cup water and mix over medium heat. Bring to a boil, then reduce the heat to low until the mixture is simmering. Stir in the rose essence, lemon juice, if using, and rose petals and simmer for about 15 minutes, until the mixture has reduced and is syrupy. Remove from the stove and cool.

DRIZZLE AND GARNISH: Once the loaf is baked, set aside to cool completely. Flip over on a serving dish. Using a toothpick, poke little holes all over the top and drizzle the rose glaze all over, allowing it to drop down the sides. Immediately sprinkle the pistachios all over the top. Let the glaze set for 5 minutes, slice, and serve or place into your tiffin. I'll admit, the longer this cake sits, the more delicious rosy juices it'll soak up. And my preferred way to eat this cake is at room temperature.

ELEVEN

The

DRINKS!

I'll let you in on a little secret: sometimes I like making drinks more than I like cooking. It's true! I feel like crafting a drink is underrated—you have to understand different fresh ingredients, dry ingredients, liquids, liquors, and techniques. There's a lot that goes into a cocktail! I've developed quite a few cocktails for various liquor brands in my time, and it's a ton of fun. I also make a custom cocktail or mocktail every time I get together with my friends or family—it's a great way to get them involved and to change up what you drink! This is my bonus chapter that's filled with five original drinks—all mocktails. They can easily be paired with a spirit if you wish, yet I wanted everyone to have a little somethin'. So, the next time you're reaching into your liquor cabinet to pour yourself a (boring) glass of wine or to make a (basic) cranberry-vodka, try making one of these instead!

Cardamom Sweet Tea Spritzer

⇒ SERVES 2 ⇐

Sweet tea is likely not everyone's cup of tea (hehe), but when paired with the slightly spicy and warm masala chai spices, it becomes a beautiful and palatable drink! I happen to love sweet tea—I'm sure you've picked up on my humongous sweet tooth by now—but I also know it can sometimes be too sweet. Confession: my mom and I used to go to the McDonald's drive-through *just* to order their gigantic 99-cent sweet tea, which no person should be drinking unless they instantly want diabetes. I don't think I need to further explain my love for sweet tea.

Which brings me to my Cardamom Sweet Tea Spritzer. This drink is a simple four ingredients (or five if you include the gin), but it's a great balance—not too sweet, not too dry—it's perfect! Give this a try with the American Comfort Tiffin. I guarantee it's a match made in heaven.

4 black tea bags

½ cup raw cane sugar

4 whole cardamom pods

1 cup ice

2 ounces gin (optional)

½ cup unsweetened nondairy creamer

Ground cardamom, for garnish

OPTIONAL GARNISHES

1 teaspoon raw cane sugar

2 pani puri puffs (see Note)

MAKE THE SWEET TEA: Place a small or medium pot over medium heat. Pour in 2 cups water and, once the water is boiling, add the tea bags, sugar, and cardamom pods. Stir to incorporate and lower the heat to medium-low. Simmer the mixture for 3 to 4 minutes. Remove from the heat, discard the tea bags, and pour the mixture into a pitcher or mason jar. Place in the fridge to cool completely.

ASSEMBLY: Divide the ice between two tall cocktail glasses and, if using gin, pour 1 ounce into each glass over the ice. Next, divide the sweet tea between the glasses. Then divide the nondairy creamer between them, pouring on top and allowing the creamer to slowly mix into the tea. If not adding the pani puri garnish (see next step), simply garnish each glass with a pinch of ground cardamom.

PANI PURI GARNISH (OPTIONAL): Place the cardamom and sugar in a bowl and mix well. Roll each puri into the cardamom-sugar mixture. Using a steel straw (or any sustainable straw), gently poke it through the middle of the puri and insert the straw into the cocktail. The puri should rest on the edge of the rim.

PORTABILITY: This drink can be easily transferred to a temperature-controlled thermos to make for a refreshing Cardamom Sweet Tea Spritzer on-the-go!

✕ ─────────────────────────

NOTE: Pani puris are made using semolina, all-purpose flour, and baking soda, then rolled into small flat rounds and fried until puffed and slightly translucent. Traditionally, pani puri puffs are hollowed out and filled with legumes, potatoes, and chilies, dipped into a sweet and spicy chutney water (called *imli pani* in Hindi), and eaten in one bite as a snack. In this instance, I am using the pani puri puffs as a sweet crunchy garnish for our Cardamom Sweet Tea Spritzer!

Saffron Lassi

⇢⟫ SERVES 2 ⟪⇠

You've had a mango lassi, I've had a mango lassi, we've all had a mango lassi. *Yawn.* But, have you ever had a saffron lassi? Aside from the fact that saffron always tints food with its beautiful yellow hue, it has the most unique taste and aroma—it's hard to compare it to anything else! Maybe that's why it's so precious (in addition to the incredibly laborious agriculture practice associated with saffron, which includes farmers picking each thread individually from saffron flowers). It really can't be replicated. I love the way this saffron lassi tastes because it reminds me of my mom's shrikhand—a strained yogurt dish, flavored with cardamom, saffron, pistachios, and sugar. It is sweet, aromatic, and not to mention, gorgeous! Make this dairy-free Saffron Lassi to bring some of those shrikhand flavors into your home.

MAKE THE SAFFRON SYRUP: In a small pot, stir together ½ cup water and the sugar and set over medium heat. Bring the mixture to a boil. Once boiling, add the saffron threads, reduce the heat to low, and simmer for 8 to 10 minutes, until the mixture reduces and thickens to a maple syrup consistency. Set aside to cool completely.

LASSI TIME: In a blender, combine the nondairy yogurt, ice, nondairy milk, and saffron syrup. Blend until smooth and creamy. Divide between two glasses and garnish with the cardamom, pistachios, and saffron threads, if using.

PORTABILITY: Lassis are enjoyed cold or at room temperature in India, so you're welcome to pack this for on-the-go. Just note that because there is a "dairy" component, I would not leave it out longer than 3 hours to be on the safe side.

¼ cup raw cane sugar

¼ teaspoon saffron threads (5 to 6 threads), plus 2 for optional garnish

1 cup full-fat nondairy yogurt, preferably coconut

½ cup ice

3 tablespoons unsweetened nondairy milk

¼ teaspoon ground cardamom, for garnish

1 tablespoon chopped unsalted pistachios, for garnish

Lemon Turmeric Cooler

⇥ SERVES 2 ⇤

This one is a simple drink, possibly even something you can incorporate in your morning routine. As you've probably heard by now, the Western world has finally discovered the benefits of turmeric and it's everywhere. Turmeric is an ancient ayurvedic spice, which means it has healing properties. Most Indian cuisine is filled with ayurvedic properties, as each natural spice and vegetable tends to have a purpose and healing property. Turmeric, in particular, has anti-inflammatory properties, immune-boosting properties, and even anticancer benefits, among many others. But the only way the properties in turmeric can be activated is through its core element: curcumin. And curcumin can only be activated when paired with a fat, such as hot coconut oil and/or a spice like black pepper. My Lemon Turmeric Cooler does just that. I tend to drink my Lemon Turmeric Cooler at the start of the day during the summer months because it's so refreshing. You can even scale the recipe up and leave a big batch in your fridge to have on a daily basis.

MAKE THE TURMERIC SOLUTION: In a small bowl, mix together the hot water and turmeric until combined. Let the turmeric dissolve into the water, creating a smooth slurry. Set aside to cool completely.

MUDDLING TIME: In a large mason jar, add the mint, lemon juice, and pepper. Using a muddler or the back of a wooden spoon, muddle together until the mint starts breaking down.

SHAKING TIME: Add half of the ice into the jar, pour in the turmeric slurry, and add the agave. Close the lid of the jar and give it a good and vigorous shake. The ice should begin melting and incorporating into the mixture. Divide between two short cocktail glasses and top with the cold seltzer water. Garnish with a sprig of mint, if you'd like, and enjoy!

PORTABILITY: This drink can easily be transferred to a temperature-controlled thermos to make for a refreshing cooler on-the-go!

- 2 tablespoons hot water
- 1 teaspoon turmeric powder
- 4 sprigs fresh mint, plus 2 for optional garnish
- Juice from ½ lemon
- ½ teaspoon freshly ground black pepper
- 1 cup ice
- 2 teaspoons light agave
- 1 (12-ounce) bottle cold seltzer water

Creamy Mango-Coconut Frozé

➤❱ SERVES 2 ❰⬅

I've been told that you can use the term "frozé" only in the context of frozen rosé wine. Well, I say, you're not the boss of me! Because this drink is certainly a "frozé," but with zero wine! Have you ever had a piña colada? Yes? Okay, good. Have you ever had a mango mojito? Yes? Okay, great! This cocktail is inspired by those two tropical treats, but with an added ayurvedic touch of turmeric and ginger, so you don't have to feel bad about drinking it. I love the combination of mango and coconut—I feel like it's a tropical classic. You can't go wrong! And the best part about this drink is that it can be made in advance and, even as it melts, it tastes delicious. Plus, there's a little trick I use in this drink with the coconut milk—go check out the recipe to find out!

MAKE THE TURMERIC SLURRY: In a small bowl, whisk together the turmeric with 1 tablespoon warm water until completely dissolved. This slurry will help the turmeric blend into the drink and eliminate any large chunks of turmeric while drinking!

FROZÉ TIME: In a blender or food processor, add the coconut milk ice cubes, mango, agave, mint, ginger, oil, and turmeric slurry. Start to blend on high and, if you have trouble (because it's frozen), add 1 tablespoon of nondairy milk and continue blending until super smooth. Add more tablespoons of nondairy milk to achieve the consistency you'd like, but it should be similar to a slushy consistency.

SERVE: Divide the frozé between two glasses and garnish each with a sprig of mint. This drink is best enjoyed immediately but, if traveling, my recommendation is to pour it into an insulated thermos along with some ice packs. Even when this drink melts, it tastes like a tropical milkshake, so you'll be sure to enjoy it!

✕ ————————————————

NOTE: To make coconut milk ice cubes, pour 2 (13.5-ounce) cans of full-fat coconut milk into two standard ice-cube trays and freeze until solid. Two trays *should* make about 2 cups of coconut milk ice cubes.

- 1 teaspoon turmeric powder
- 2 cups coconut milk ice cubes (see Note)
- 2 cups frozen mango chunks
- 2 teaspoons light agave, or to taste
- 4 sprigs fresh mint, plus 2 more for garnish
- 1 (½-inch) piece fresh ginger, peeled and grated
- 1 teaspoon coconut oil
- 1 or more tablespoons nondairy milk (optional)

Unicorn Rose Refresher

➤➤ SERVES 2 ⟵⟵

Unicorns are real. It's a fact, okay? I don't make these things up! If you don't believe me, just make this drink. There is a magical *au naturale* color-changing effect in my Unicorn Rose Refresher, which proves that unicorns exist, duh! Now you're probably thinking, what is this crazy chef talking about? What I am referring to are butterfly pea flowers. Yes, this completely natural Southeast Asian flower is equipped with a highly pigmented dye that, when activated by an acid, for example lemon, will change its color to pink or purple. How cool is that? So of course, I had to develop a drink just so we can have some fun! Your kids are going to love this, or you will if you're like me, because I'm a giant kid and absolutely love this! Plus, it pairs so beautifully with rose. This is definitely a video- and photo-worthy recipe. But isn't everything in my book? Ha!

3 to 4 tablespoons raw cane sugar, or to taste

2 tablespoons whole dried butterfly pea flowers

½ teaspoon rose essence or rose water

Rose ice cubes (see Note)

1 (12-ounce) can cold sparkling water

2 lemon wedges

2 ounces good-quality gin (optional, if you want a cocktail)

MAKE THE TEA: Place a small pot over medium-low heat and add 2½ cups water with the sugar, butterfly pea flowers, and rose essence. Stir and bring it to a boil, then reduce the heat to low and simmer for 3 to 4 minutes, until the sugar has dissolved and the butterfly pea flowers have bled all of their blue color. Strain into a pitcher through a fine-mesh strainer. Set aside to cool completely.

SERVE AND SEE MAGIC: Place the rose ice cubes into two tall cocktail glasses. Pour the cooled butterfly-rose tea into each glass. Top with the cold sparkling water and then squeeze a wedge of lemon into each glass and watch the magic of the blue tea turning pink! Stir with a straw and drink up.

COCKTAIL: If making a cocktail, add the rose ice cubes to each glass and pour 1 ounce gin into each glass over the cubes. Then pour in the cooled butterfly-rose tea and squeeze in the fresh lemon. Stir and enjoy!

PORTABILITY: This drink can be easily transferred to a temperature-controlled thermos to make for a refreshing Unicorn Refresher on-the-go. As the temperature picks up, the rose ice cubes will melt, and the rose petals will freely float in your Unicorn Rose Refresher and are 100 percent edible! It's a summertime favorite for me!

✕ ——————————————————

NOTE: To make rose ice cubes, place 1 to 2 dried rose petals in each cavity of an ice cube tray. Gently pour in the water and place in the freezer to set completely. Keep in the freezer until ready to serve.

GLOSSARY

This glossary is meant to be used as a reference guide while you cook your way through *The Modern Tiffin*. I wish I could list every ingredient here—including definitions and outlining some of my favorite brands for you to use as your ingredient "bible" or, I should say, ingredient "Bhagavad Gita" since I'm a practicing Hindu. But that would almost be a book in and of itself. So instead, I'm including those ingredients that may be unfamiliar to you or are special to Indian cuisine—and you can find the rest on my website, chefpriyanka.com (as well as brands specific to India and the UK). As a rule of thumb, I always work with unsalted, no-salt-added, or low-sodium products. I (and you should, too) want to have the utmost control over my cooking and what I'm putting into my body.

BLUE CORNFLOWERS
Edible and native to Europe, these are generally sold as a dry flower and have a bright blue hue that makes them particularly pop on cakes and desserts. They are available online or in specialty bake shops.

BUTTERFLY PEA FLOWERS
These are dried whole flowers of the *Clitoria ternatea* plant. They originate in Southeast Asia and have a natural blue hue, which emits into boiled water and changes color with the addition of acid, like fresh lemon. Butterfly pea flowers are considered an herbal tea and are caffeine-free, with minimal flavor.

CHICKPEA FLOUR
Also known as gram or besan flour within Indian cuisine and culture, this is finely ground dried chickpeas. A great source of protein and potassium, besan flour is used throughout India in sweet, savory, and snack-y dishes. A staple in many batters and street food dishes, chickpea flour is thick in nature; if you are making the pancake-style recipe on page 50, the batter needs to be thin (almost a crepe-batter consistency) in order for it to cook all the way through. Chickpea flour is readily available in supermarkets, but the most economically friendly and best-quality chickpea flour is available at Indian grocery stores, specifically brands such as Swad and Laxmi.

JAGGERY

An unrefined cane sugar, or what we call *bella* in Kannada, jaggery contains many more nutrient and mineral properties than processed sugar. It is a "noncentrifugal" cane sugar, which means the naturally occurring molasses and nutrients aren't spun out. Jaggery is indigenous to India and Africa and used extensively in sweet and savory cooking throughout India. Blocks of jaggery are available at Indian supermarkets or online.

MANGOES

There are more than a dozen varieties of mangoes available in supermarkets and more than five hundred varieties all over the world, including raw mango, which is delicious in cold dishes and as a salad. And most, if not all, are indigenous to India. The mangoes I prefer to use are Kent mangoes, which is a strain of mango developed in southern Florida. Kent mangoes are big in size, juicy with a soft flesh, and fiberless. These characteristics make it easy to cook with and consume. Kent mangoes are available in season or can be ordered online from tropicalfruitbox.com.

NONDAIRY "DAIRY"

There is a tremendous number of nondairy "dairy" items available across supermarkets. As the demand for vegan items increases (due to the increase in adopting a vegan lifestyle), the number of brands producing vegan products is increasing, which is a fabulous thing! There are several styles, brands, and price points available across supermarkets and online. Below I outline the nondairy "dairy" items that I use throughout this cookbook, as well as some of my preferred brands.

BUTTER: Vegan butter is usually made with a combination of nuts or oats and oils. I prefer a stick-style unsalted vegan butter for baking (it's equivalent to dairy butter and easy to measure), like Earth Balance or Flora Plant-based Butter brands. For cooking, I prefer a spreadable butter made from oat milk, to minimize any residual flavors that a cashew- or soy-based butter would have. I prefer Miyoko's, Califia, or Earth Balance brands.

CHEESE (FETA, GOUDA, CHEDDAR, PEPPER JACK, MOZZARELLA, CREAM CHEESE): There are hundreds of vegan cheeses available on the market and in all different styles. Throughout this cookbook, I use sliced and shredded cheeses. Most of these cheeses are made with a base of coconut and/or nuts along with tapioca flour or potato starch and coconut or vegetable oils. Some of my preferred brands include Field Roast Sliced Cheese and Shreds, Violife Foods Shreds, Esti Feta and Mozzarella, Follow Your Heart Gouda Slices, and Miyoko's Shreds. Another ingredient I use heavily is vegan cream cheese—it's a great way to thicken sauces, adds moisture and creaminess to baked goods, and is perfect for bagels. My preferred brands are Tofutti and Kite Hill Foods.

COCONUT MILK: Made from blending down coconut meat to a pulp and straining out the liquid, pure coconut milk contains just coconut and is generally sold in cans. I prefer this kind of coconut milk for baking and making drinks. But for drinking casually and using in savory cooking recipes, I prefer using over-the-shelf carton coconut milk, as it's diluted with water and does not have a strong coconut flavor. Some of my preferred brands are Califia, So Delicious, and Thai Kitchen (for canned coconut milk).

CREAMER/HALF-AND-HALF: Vegan creamer is generally made with a coconut cream and/or nut milk and soy milk. There are many flavors available (which are perfect for coffee and tea), but there are also unsweetened plain varieties. I use those for adding body and creaminess to sauces, gravies, soups, pasta, and much more. My preferred brands include Califia, So Delicious, and Elmhurst.

MAYONNAISE: Vegan mayonnaise can be made with tofu or aquafaba (chickpea water), lemon, oil, salt, vinegar, and sometimes Dijon mustard. It has a similar consistency and taste to traditional egg-based mayonnaise and can be used in the same manner. Some of my preferred brands are Sir Kensington's, Follow Your Heart, and Hellmann's (yes, they make vegan mayonnaise!).

NUT MILK: It is exactly what it says—nuts that have been blended down to a pulp, combined with water, and strained. Nut milk comes in all nut varieties— almond, cashew, macadamia, hazelnut, walnut, and more. My preferred is almond milk for regular drinking and cooking, and macadamia milk for coffee and decadent dishes. I always purchase plain unsweetened nut milk to minimize the intake of sugar. Some of my preferred brands include Califia, Elmhurst, So Delicious, and Ripple. Try to look for milks that have added calcium and protein (they are mostly legume-based).

OAT MILK: This is also exactly what it says—oats that have been blended down to a pulp, combined with water, and strained. I prefer oat milk for drinking and cooking over nut milk, because it has protein (naturally from oats), is creamy, and has less flavor, so it's perfect for savory dishes. My preferred brands are Oatly and Califia (with protein).

SOUR CREAM: Vegan sour cream is generally made from tofu and/or cashews, vinegar, and vegetable-based oils. It has a similar consistency and taste to dairy sour cream. I use vegan sour cream for sauces, chutneys, and to top off my delicious Mexican dishes. My preferred brands are Kite Hill Foods and Tofutti.

YOGURT: I prefer to use coconut, almond, or oat yogurt.

POMEGRANATE (RED)

Indigenous to present-day Iran and India and considered an ancient fruit, there are more than a dozen varieties of pomegranate, but the most commonly available is the red, sweet-tart Wonderful pomegranate with pink-red seeds. Pomegranates contain polyphenols and are high in antioxidants, which offer heart-healthy and anticancer benefits. I recommend purchasing whole pomegranates, readily available in supermarkets, as it is economically efficient to do so and minimizes the use of plastic that shelled pomegranate seeds come in. Pomegranates are generally in season from September to November in the States.

RICE (ARBORIO)

An Italian short-grain rice that is used primarily to make risotto, arborio has a consistency and plumpness that is perfect for risotto's creamy texture but requires a minimum of 35 to 40 minutes to cook. Arborio is named after the town Arborio in Piedmont, Italy.

RICE (BASMATI)

A long-grain rice indigenous to India, basmati has a distinct texture and taste that makes it hard to substitute. It works well in both savory and sweet dishes, and depending on desired consistency, basmati rice can be cooked to be fluffy or what we call in our home "midgy"—which is a bit softer and mushier. The best-quality basmati rice is available at Indian supermarkets or online and I highly recommend buying an Indian imported brand, like Swad or Laxmi.

RICE (SPANISH BOMBA)

A Spanish short-grain rice primarily used for paella, Spanish bomba rice is similar to arborio rice, which can be used as a substitute. Bomba rice is short and plump in texture, which allows for a creamy and hearty product and requires a minimum of 35 to 40 minutes to cook.

ROSE ESSENCE/
WATER

Similarly to vanilla extract, rose essence is made by submerging rose petals in a clear spirit (like vodka) and setting aside for at least a year for the alcohol to dissipate and the liquid to pick up the rose flavor. Rose essence is incredibly strong in flavor, so a little goes a long way. Rose water is made using a steam distillation method and results in a softer rose flavor. Both products are readily available in Indian grocery stores and online, and are used primarily in desserts and drinks.

ROSE PETALS
(DRIED)

Most roses are edible. Why most? Because only roses that are organic and pesticide-free can be consumed. Fresh rose petals are separated from the stem and air-dried in the sun or even lightly toasted in an oven to create dried rose petals. These petals provide a subtle hint of rose flavor and add a distinct artistic quality to dishes. The best dried rose petals are available at Indian supermarkets or online.

SEMOLINA

A coarse ground wheat used for a variety of savory dishes in Indian cuisine, semolina is a close and great substitute for Indian sooji, which is a finely ground purified wheat, mainly used for desserts and pudding-style dishes. Semolina is readily available in supermarkets, and if the white variety is available, then that is preferred.

SEV

Sev is a commonly used (and consumed) Indian snack that is eaten alone or used as a garnish on many dishes. Sev is made out of chickpeas, specifically chickpea flour, and is available in thick, medium, and thin varieties. I recommend purchasing the thin variety for the recipes in this cookbook. The best-quality thin sev in the States is available at Sukhadia's; otherwise any Indian brand of thin sev at an Indian supermarket or online will do, too.

SPICES

Here is a list of spices used throughout this cookbook—some are dry and some are fresh.

AMCHUR POWDER: Mango powder, made from raw mango that has been dried, amchur powder has a sweet and tangy flavor. It is widely used in Indian masalas (seasonings), chutneys, and drinks. It adds an umami flavor. Amchur powder is available at all Indian supermarkets and online. My preferred brands are MDH, Swad, and Laxmi.

BLACK MUSTARD SEEDS: Among the same family of plants as yellow mustard seeds, these are not as common in Western cooking. Black mustard seeds originate from North Africa and Asia. They have a spicy and strong aroma and, when cooked in hot oil, their flavors are released. Black mustard seeds are very commonly used in South Indian, Goan, and Central Indian cuisines and as an ingredient in pickling. Yellow mustard seeds cannot be substituted for black mustard seeds, as the flavors and textures differ.

CARDAMOM PODS: Thought to have originated in Asia, specifically South India amid tropical climates, there are early mentions of cardamom in ayurvedic and Hindu literatures. It comes from a fruit, and the pods are a green shell housing the black cardamom seed inside. Pods are used whole across Indian and Middle Eastern cooking, especially in rice dishes. Using the whole cardamom pods emits a delicate cardamom flavor, without overpowering the dish, and is great for long-cooking dishes (like biryani and tahdig). There are also medicinal characteristics of cardamom, commonly used to regulate sugar levels for diabetes patients and to lower high cholesterol.

CARDAMOM SEEDS: Found inside the cardamom pod, these black seeds can be easily ground in a mortar and pestle and then incorporated into dishes and as a garnish. Cardamom has a distinct earthy, citrusy, and slightly floral flavor. It is used in both sweet and savory dishes and commonly appears among Indian masalas (seasonings). Cardamom has a distinct and strong flavor, so a little goes a long way.

CHAAT MASALA: A popular Indian spice mixture used across sweet, savory, and drink recipes. It is generally a combination of amchur powder, cumin powder, coriander powder, red chili powder, black salt, dried ginger, black pepper, and hing. Chaat masala has the ability to accentuate sweet, spicy, and aromatic flavors on a fruit, in a savory dish, or even on top of a drink. It is commonly sprinkled on top of *peru* (white guava), cucumbers, into *chaats* (street food dishes made of legumes, crispies, and chutneys), and on top of cold drinks like *nimbu paani* (lemon-lime water). My preferred brands are MDH Chunky Chaat Masala and Badshah Chat Masala, available at Indian supermarkets or online.

CURRY LEAVES (FRESH): Completely unrelated to curry powder, curry leaves originate in India on a subtropical tree. The leaves are harvested fresh and used across Indian cooking, but primarily in Central and Southern Indian cooking. They have a distinct spicy and citrusy flavor that cannot be substituted by any other spice. Curry leaves are generally cooked in hot oil and are distinct for "popping" and "shimmering," allowing the flavors to emit into the respective dish. Curry leaves can also be fried and served crispy, and are used in a variety of snack dishes. They have various healing and medicinal properties and are used as an ayurvedic ingredient. Packed with fiber, calcium, iron, and vitamins, curry leaves have been thought to improve heart function and enliven hair and skin. They are available fresh in Indian grocery stores and online.

FLEUR DE SEL: Originating in France and translating to "flower of the sea," both sea salt and fleur de sel are from seawater, but fleur de sel is the crystals that rise to the top in the evaporation process, whereas sea salt is what is left after evaporating all the seawater. Fleur de sel tends to be thinner and flakier with a floral taste. It is generally used as a garnish and pairs well with caramel and chocolate.

GARAM MASALA: This commonly used Indian spice blend is made of warm spices like cloves, cinnamon, and nutmeg. Garam masala is primarily used in North Indian/Punjabi-style cooking and adds a depth and layers of flavors without having to cook a dish for hours upon hours. Here is my simple recipe for garam masala that you can make from scratch. This will keep up to 6 months in an airtight jar in a cool, dark, and dry place.

MIX TOGETHER:

- 1 tablespoon ground cumin
- 1 heaping teaspoon ground coriander
- 1 heaping teaspoon ground cinnamon
- ½ teaspoon ground cardamom
- ½ teaspoon freshly ground black pepper
- ¼ heaping teaspoon ground cloves
- ¼ heaping teaspoon ground nutmeg

GREEN CHILIES (FRESH): There are several varieties of green chilies around the world. In this cookbook, I use Indian green chilies, which are small deep-green shiny chilies with long stems. They are very spicy, full of seeds, and have a distinct flavor that combines well with Indian dishes. They are sold in bulk at Indian grocery stores. A close substitute is green chile de arbol from Mexico or serrano chili peppers.

HABANERO PEPPERS (FRESH): Originating in Mexico, these peppers are simply hot. They have a distinct orange or red color and are round and plump with a thin stem. Their flavor has hints of citrus and floral notes, which combine well with Mexican and Latin flavors. The habanero is on the upper echelon of the Scoville scale but is not the hottest—thanks to Carolina Reapers and the Trinidad Moruga Scorpion.

HING (ASAFETIDA): Derived from the fennel plant and originating from present-day Iran and Afghanistan, hing is equivalent to an Indian umami taste and a little goes a long way! Many regions of India cook with hing, especially Jains (who traditionally do not consume onions and garlic), because it adds a distinct flavor and aroma that rounds out a dish. Hing can be found in Indian supermarkets or online. My preferred brand is LG Hing (a white bottle with black and red writing).

KASHMIRI RED CHILIES (DRIED WHOLE): These large, wide red chilies have a wrinkled surface (from drying) and originate in Kashmir. They have a medium spice level, but the unique characteristic is the bright red hue that Kashmiri chili adds to a dish. Dried Kashmiri chilies are available in Indian supermarkets and online.

PEQUIN CHILI PEPPERS: Originating in the American Southwest and Mexico, these are small red dried chilies. Pequin refers to the "small" size, but they are very spicy in flavor. They have notes of citrus and combine well in salsas, soups, sautés, and many more Mexican dishes. Dried pequin chili peppers are available in supermarkets and online.

RED CHILIES (DRIED WHOLE): There are several varieties of dried red chilies, but I use Indian dried chilies, which are long, thick dark-red chilies. They originated in Mexico and were brought over to India by Portuguese traders. They have a very spicy and slightly nutty flavor and are used in fresh dishes and snacks, and ground up in chutneys. India is now considered one of the biggest cultivators of dried red chilies, which can be found in Indian supermarkets or online. A substitute is dried chile de arbol.

RED CHILI POWDER: I often use two varieties of chili powders: spicy Indian red chili powder and Kashmiri chili powder. Spicy Indian red chili powder is made from finely ground dried red chili peppers; a similar chili powder and acceptable substitute is cayenne pepper. Kashmiri chili powder is made from finely ground dried Kashmiri chilies, which have a bright red hue and are used to add color and mild spice to dishes. Both are available in Indian supermarkets or online.

SAFFRON THREADS (FRESH): The stigma of the saffron flower, the threads are harvested by being individually picked, which explains the high price tag. Saffron originates in the Mediterranean, Asia Minor, and Iran but is now also cultivated in Morocco, India, and Greece. Saffron has a delicate flavor and aroma, but it is mainly used for the color it emits—a beautiful yellow hue. Saffron is available in all supermarkets, but I recommend purchasing it at an Indian grocery store, which will have lower prices, better quality, and you can buy in bulk. Saffron should be stored in the fridge for up to six months—it is a fresh ingredient.

SAMBAL CHILI PASTE: A popular Indonesian chili sauce made of red chilies, garlic, ginger, lime, scallions/onions, and palm sugar, this is a great paste to use in sauces, dips, and aioli. My preferred brand is Sambal Oelek.

TURMERIC POWDER: One of the oldest spices, turmeric dates back to Vedic culture in India and has ayurvedic and religious (Hindu) significance. Turmeric is made from fresh turmeric root by boiling and drying the root and grinding it down to a powder. Turmeric is bright yellow and has many natural healing and medicinal properties, including anticancer and anti-inflammatory properties. It adds color and aroma to food, but too much can make a dish taste bitter or woody. Turmeric is available widely across supermarkets, but I recommend purchasing from an Indian supermarket for optimal price and quality.

TAMARIND

A fruit that grows on trees and is indigenous to Africa and India, the protective outer shells of the tamarind are opened to reveal a sweet and tart, slightly sticky, and dark brown fibrous fruit. This fruit is cooked down with water to a concentrate and made into a chutney, commonly known as tamarind or sweet chutney, which includes tamarind, sugar (date or jaggery), water, ginger, red chili powder, garlic, cardamom, cinnamon, and cloves. Tamarind chutneys are available in Indian supermarkets, in some mainstream supermarkets, and online. Some of my preferred brands include Swad and Deep. The key is to look for a thick consistency, a shiny brown color, and a balance of sweet and tart flavors.

RESOURCES

This short list is easily accessed if you live in the States, and includes the resources where I regularly purchase my fruits and vegetables. Most of these establishments are small businesses, minority-owned, and immigrant-owned. It is important that we strive to support fresh produce that is in season to protect the species of the crop and consume it at a stage that is the most nutrient-rich. It is equally important to support businesses that are striving to make the world more sustainable and make fresh food accessible to the masses.

PATEL BROTHERS/ PATEL CASH & CARRY

My family has been going to this Indian immigrant–owned small business for years. They have fifty-seven locations across the States and provide all of the ingredients I outline in this cookbook—and they are inexpensive, may I add! If you live in the States, check to see if you live by a Patel Cash & Carry; you will be in produce heaven, I promise! Otherwise, check out patelbrothers.com.

FARMERS' MARKETS

Whenever possible, I try to support my local farmers' markets. Local farmers plant and harvest produce when it's in season and grow some of the freshest, best-tasting, and most nutrient-rich produce. Most are small businesses and, by supporting a farmers' market, we are supporting the long-term sustainable growth of farming agriculture and minimizing the need for GMO (genetically modified organism) products. Farmers' markets also sell in bulk and are inexpensive.

FRUIT SUPPLIERS

There has been an increase in tropical fruit suppliers in the States, like Tropical Fruit Box and Miami Fruit. These farmers are small businesses, minority-owned, and in the case of Tropical Fruit Box, female-owned businesses that are providing access to fresh fruits all over the country. They have developed their own micro farms and partner with local farmers in tropical climates (mainly Florida) to sustainably grow tropical fruit to ship across the country. This makes it possible for someone in New York City in the middle of January to get ripe mangoes, without disrupting the crop or modifying it in any way. It ensures the most nutrient-rich and best-tasting fruit. These suppliers are not cheap, but in supporting their businesses, we are supporting a sustainable way of farming and fruit production that can eventually be made available to the masses. Check out tropicalfruitbox.com and miamifruit.org online.

URBAN FARMERS

Over the past several years, there has been a boom in urban farms in the States, especially New York City. Urban farmers take small spaces in urban areas (rooftops, basements, abandoned landmasses) and create year-round, sustainable, crop-producing farms. They mainly use hydroponic technology, which requires little to no soil, recycles water, and grows within a greenhouse, to produce fresh, pesticide-free crops. These urban farms enable high-density urban areas to access fresh, nutrient-rich, and completely chemical-free vegetables and other produce regularly. This style of farming breaks the mold of traditional agriculture. Some of my favorite urban farms include Gotham Greens (gothamgreens.com), Farm One (farm.one), and Bowery Farming (boweryfarming.com).

ACKNOWLEDGMENTS

I wish I could pretend I'm Superwoman and say that I whipped this beautiful and honest cookbook up on my own, but that is, oh, so not the case! I have had so many people in my community and network supporting me and cheering me on, and every one of them has helped in bringing this dream of a cookbook to life! So here are all the people I'd like to acknowledge.

THE SWAT TEAM

None of this would have been possible, literally, without THE Swat Team. Also known as the magicians who helped bring my longtime vision to life, put up with my million and one questions, and executed all the crazy ideas I had.

First to my agent, Andrea Cascardi: Thank you SO much for believing in me since day one, being persistent with the industry (even after rejections in the beginning), working with me so honestly, and ultimately being the launchpad to changing my life in the culinary industry. A thank-you isn't enough, in my opinion! And also thank you to our alma mater, Boston University, because without their feature on me in *Bostonia* magazine, you would have never discovered me!

Second to my editors, Anja Schmidt and Justin Schwartz: Thank you for being patient, holding my hand through my first book, letting me tell my story how I intended to, and believing in my dream. Oh, and for kindly correcting my subpar grammar, ha!

Third to art director Patrick Sullivan and designer Matthew Ryan: Thank you for being open to my culture and its nuances, bringing my colorful and at times crazy vision to life, and working hand-in-hand with me to make my cookbook dreams come true—you truly are the magicians of this group! I don't know how you do it, but I have so much to learn from you both.

Last, but certainly not least, my powerful, talented, all-female group of creatives—Melissa Hom, Jennifer Xue, Julia Choi-Rodriguez, and Debbie Wee: Thank you for physically bringing all of my food, travels, vision, and ideas to life, by recognizing the subtle detail to cultural nuances, picking up on my personality traits, capturing my family moments, and making the best use of our home and kitchen there ever has been! Seriously, there is so much talent among you all, I feel like you can conquer the world.

CULINARY MENTORS

To Hetal Vasavada and Bryant Terry: Thank you for being honest friends, fans, supporters, and mentors in the culinary and publishing spaces. I wouldn't have learned the ropes of publishing and making my voice known in both industries if it weren't for you. Thank you so much, and I can't wait to take charge and continue making our voices, culture, and food known in the culinary and media industries in the future!

And it goes without saying, but thanks to my mom (Maa) and my dad (daaad is how I really say it at home), who have been a tremendous influence on my pursuit of the culinary arts, my understanding of our Indian heritage and culture, and the more-than-honest feedback that is consistently provided whenever I cook. Not to mention, my natural culinary "chops" are owed to both and the creativity specifically from Maa!

RECIPE TESTERS

No matter what stage you're in with your culinary career, asking someone to make one of your recipes is almost always nerve-racking and exciting. I had many friends and family members of all backgrounds, all parts of the world, and all cooking expertise levels test and provide feedback on all of the delicious recipes included in this book. And without their feedback, I wouldn't have been able to make them just perfect for you. So, to the list below, thank you for all your time, effort, and cooking chops:

Alex Hodara and family,
New York City

Amber Merhaut and family,
Pennsylvania

Drs. Puja and Padam Bhatia
and Opaline, Miami

Dr. Appasaheb and Manjula Naik,
New York City

Gauravi and Gautham Killampalli,
Massachusetts

Hetal Vasavada and family,
California

Jack Leonard, Hong Kong

Janice Ye and family, Massachusetts

Jay Shetty and family,
New York City

Jeanne Reilly and family,
Pennsylvania

Jennifer Xue, New York City

Joseph Naimoli and family,
New York City

Kirti Naik and Kiran Srikant,
New York City

Megan Kothari and family,
New York City

Rachel Reilly, Singapore

Vesselina Pentcheva and
family, Illinois

Zarmina Khankhel,
Massachusetts

**FOOD
SUPPLIERS**

Many of the recipes for my cookbook would not have been complete without the generous support and supply of fresh goods from some of my favorite minority-owned small businesses. Thank you, Patel Brothers of Edison, New Jersey—you have been a staple resource for my family for many years and without your fresh banana leaves, select produce, and family tiffins, we would not have been able to bring some of my dishes to life!

Tropical Fruit Box of Miami, Florida—you ladies are bad*ss! Thank you so much for supplying the fresh Kent mangoes and habaneros all the way from Miami to my home. I love what your business stands for and how you empower other female, minority-owned small businesses. You all are amazing!

TASTEMADE

Thank you to Emily Sweet, Lindsay Farber, and Raj Rawal for being tremendous supporters of my cookbook—when I didn't even have an agent yet—and for making my voice known and embracing the vegan diet and lifestyle. And for being the platform for my first major original hosted TV show. I can't wait to make more magic!

FORBES

A tremendous thank-you to Leslie Kelly and Adrian Miller for recognizing my place in the culinary and social media spaces and for being the first major publication to talk about my debut cookbook!

THE NAIKS

Let's be honest, I wouldn't even *be* here without my family—literally and figuratively. My family is not the typical Indian family, as in no one forced me to become a doctor, lawyer, or engineer. Heck, I don't even have a graduate school degree, which is rare for a first-generation South Asian woman! My family, specifically Dad and Maa, have been uber supportive of my passion for cooking since the beginning. They've been pushing me to pursue cooking, appear on TV, and write a book for years. And the only reason I'm a fantastic self-taught cook (I'm totally modest, as you can see) is because of my parents. Both of them, especially Maa, have taught me a lot of what I know, instilled our culture in me and my sisters, and injected us with the travel bug at a very early age.

My older sisters, Kirti and Puja, have equally been strong influences on my cooking talent and career. From finding the best restaurants to go to, to travel adventures, and learning different cuisines to cook, they have been on this journey with me since the start (they didn't really have a choice, considering I became their little leech starting June 6, 1988).

And, of course, my brother-in-law, Padam, and my two little nieces, Kiran (watch out—this one may be a future baker extraordinaire!) and Opaline (another chef in training!), have contributed to my journey and my first cookbook. Without their unconditional support, love, and critical feedback, I would not be the cook I am today and, finally, an author.

So, thank you, and all the love from your grumpy little (but not so little anymore) sloth, Pittu.

INDEX

Page numbers in *italics* refer to photos.

ABOUT THE PHOTOGRAPHER

MELISSA HOM is a food, restaurant, interior, and portrait photographer born and raised in New York City. She was named *New York* magazine's first staff photographer in its forty-plus-year history in 2006. She is known to add fresh, original visuals to the magazine and website, which receives over 13.7 million viewers monthly. Melissa also works as an independent photographer and works on artistic, commercial, and documentary-style photo projects. She received honorable mentions from the International Photography Awards in 2009 and 2008. Her client list ranges from Blender to *Glamour*, *GQ* to *National Geographic*, Moët Hennessy to Pearson Education, *TV Guide* to *Wine Spectator*, *Playboy* to the *New York Times*, and many more. She is a graduate of New York University with a journalism degree and is self-taught in photography. Curiosity is her greatest motivator, and her passions are people, moments, ideas, flavors, and the paths to capturing them.

ABOUT THE ILLUSTRATOR

JENNIFER "JENN" XUE is a self-taught illustrator. Despite having a degree in cognitive neuroscience and working full-time in marketing for a tech company, she has always had a passion for art. Jenn has been drawing for as long as she remembers, leaving behind trails of doodle-covered notes and napkins anywhere she went. She is inspired by her favorite pastimes: cooking, traveling, and uncovering neighborhood gems in NYC. She loves to use fun and bright colors to highlight the beauty in simple, everyday objects and places. Jenn mainly works in digital mediums, but also enjoys painting with watercolors and gouache. When she isn't working or pursuing her hobbies, she loves to bake and immerses herself in watching videos of cute animals on the internet. Jenn currently lives in Brooklyn, New York, with her partner, Alberto, and cat, Lila.

ABOUT THE AUTHOR

PRIYANKA NAIK is a self-taught Indian vegan cook, Food Network champion, Quibi *Dishmantled* winner, and *TODAY* show featured chef. She is a food and TV personality, who hosts "Dish It Healthy with Priyanka Naik," a Tastemade original, clean-eating food show on Food Network Kitchen. An avid traveler who's been to nearly forty countries, her globally inspired original recipes have been featured on her blog ChefPriyanka.com, on her digital series "Cook with Chef Pri at 3" hosted on IGTV, and are incorporated into her regular speaking appearances. She has been featured on the *TODAY* show and CNN, and in *Bon Appétit*, The Kitchn, *Glamour*, *Forbes*, *GQ*, *The Beet*, Well + Good, Medium.com, and more. She has partnered with several brands, including Spotify, Coca-Cola, Amazon, and Uniqlo, for campaigns. In addition to vegan cooking, Priyanka equally concentrates on sustainability, zero-waste cooking, sustainable fashion, and supporting women-owned, minority-owned small businesses.

Priyanka is first-generation Indian American, raised on Staten Island, New York, and has two elder sisters. Her Indian heritage is very important to her cooking style and lifestyle, so much so that she even learned her native language of Kannada before English and weaves Indian elements into all of her original vegan cooking. She attributes her devotion to her Indian roots and passion for Indian food to her loving and supportive parents. Priyanka attended Boston University, earning a bachelor of arts in economics. She has had a full career in consulting, data science, and technology, holding positions at Publicis Groupe, Bloomberg LP, Condé Nast, and Twitter. She currently lives in Manhattan and spends a LOT of time in her kitchen.